Pella Dutch

Pella Dutch

*The Portrait of a Language and Its Use
in One of Iowa's Ethnic Communities*

PHILIP E. WEBBER

Iowa State University Press / Ames

To my quiver full of arrows

—PSALMS 127:4–5

PHILIP E. WEBBER is Professor of German in the Division of Cross-Cultural Studies at Central College, where he currently chairs the Department of German, is cochair of Linguistics, and regularly teaches Dutch.

Composed by Iowa State University Press from author-provided disks
Printed in the United States of America

First edition, 1988

Grateful acknowledgment is made of a major publication subsidy by the AEGON Insurance Group of The Hague, parent corporation of Life Investors of Cedar Rapids, Iowa.

Library of Congress Cataloging-in-Publication Data

Webber, Philip E., 1944–
    Pella Dutch.
    Bibliography: p.
    Includes index.
    1. Dutch language—Dialects—Iowa—Pella. 2. English language—Foreign elements—Dutch. 3. Bilingualism—Iowa—Pella. 4. Languages in contact—Iowa—Pella. 5. Pella (Iowa)—Languages. 6. Dutch—Iowa—Pella. 7. Pella (Iowa)—Social life and customs.
I. Title.
PF891.W43   1988   439.3'1777783   87–35395
ISBN 0–8138–0079–X

CONTENTS

PREFACE

THE purpose of this study is to present the fruits of close to a decade's research in which language was not merely a tool, but rather the thematic focus of investigation by a participant-observer into the life of one of Iowa's major ethnic communities. While I have thoroughly enjoyed the archival and historical research attendant to the task, my approach to an understanding of this Dutch-American community has been primarily through personal contacts and interviews. I readily concede that the record of Pella's past has by no means been fully investigated, and in some cases virtually cries for attention. Still more urgent, in my own view, has been the need to work at once with those human resources who, as speakers of Pella Dutch, are the final bearers of a link to the past that cannot be adequately reconstructed at a future date. It is sobering to witness death and the ravages of age irreparably diminishing the circle of willing and capable sources whom I have come to know as friends and associates in this undertaking.

Consistent with a desire to let this be the speakers' account of Pella Dutch, I have allowed the chronological and topical scope of the work to be that which has emerged naturally out of direct contact with members of the community. I have limited myself primarily to the period remembered by living individuals, hence approximately the early 1900s to the present; when I delve into an earlier period, it is to elucidate ideas and concerns expressed by local residents.

In terms of specific topics, I soon discovered (and frequently saw the fact reconfirmed) that there were certain points the townsfolk wished to make, and no gentle (or even rather firm) attempts on my part at redirecting the course of inquiry would allow me to substitute my own agenda for theirs. As a result, language investigation became more than an end in itself; it served as a means of gaining access to a broad variety of background, freely shared throughout this monograph, on the social milieu in which Dutch is spoken in Pella and surrounding communities. While the thematic focus of my research was sociolinguistic, the scope of areas it came to encompass was much broader. If at any point it appears that I am citing information of a less complimentary nature, it is done solely in the interest of transmitting a representative and reasonably complete record of the testimony given by the speaker pool, and by no means in an attempt to dip into any less savory elements that may be simmering behind Pella's tranquil facade.

Some persons assured me they would be delighted to have their name associated with the ideas they expressed; others pleaded that they remain anonymous. It seems fairest to let all receive my sincere, open thanks, and likewise to let all remain unnamed. Met genoegen zeg ik mijn hartelijke dank!

I owe a particular debt of gratitude for careful reading of my preliminary draft to Prof. Kees Boot of Dordt College, and to a host of colleagues too numerous to name (and not least of all the library and technical support staffs at Central College) for assistance great and small. Dr. Jo Daan of Barchem, the Netherlands, who recently published a major work on the Dutch of ethnic enclaves such as Pella, supplied me with ideas and documentation that I scarcely would have encountered in the normal course of investigation carried out in this country. Mr. Ken Vander Linden of Pella helped me to gain access to a number of key historic photographs. I am indebted for both direct project support and for valuable assistance in collateral areas of work to the Trustees of Central College for a research sabbatical in the spring of 1983, as well as to the Central College Faculty Committee on Research and Development, the Iowa Humanities Board/National Endowment for the Humanities, the American Folklife Center of the Library of Congress, and the Mellon Foundation/University House of the University of Iowa.

Publication of the fruits of this research was enhanced by a grant from the AEGON Insurance Group of The Hague and its subsidiary, Life Investors of Cedar Rapids, Iowa.

PART ONE

The People

Many early settlers preferred physical environments reminiscent of their home regions in the Netherlands, while adopting exterior and interior conventions that were distinctly American.

Photo by Les Sadler, courtesy of Ken Vander Linden

Photo by Les Sadler, courtesy of Ken Vander Linden

Pella and Its Speakers

A T the time of the 1980 census, Iowa claimed the highest percentage of residents with Dutch ancestry (6.5 percent) of any state. True, a number of other states boast of older settlements, or of larger overall Dutch-American populations than Iowa's 188,357 residents with roots in the Netherlands. None, however, may point to as great a relative current impact by the Dutch on overall patterns of ethnicity within the state as does Iowa, where Pella stands out as the oldest Dutch-American colony, and the one which has spawned, directly or indirectly, the state's other major centers of Dutch-American life.[1]

Pella is a community of approximately 8000 residents in northeastern Marion County. Founded in 1847 by religious separatists under the leadership of Reverend H. P. Scholte, the town takes its name from a first-century A.D. Palestinian city of refuge for persecuted Christians.[2]

In Iowa, Pella is known for its annual Tulip Time festival and as the home of the Rolscreen Corporation (makers of the Pella window) and Vermeer Manufacturing (a major producer of farm implements). Visitors to Pella will recall the Dutch architectural motifs on its uptown buildings, and the pervasive presence of Dutch names on commercial establishments.[3]

Those who live in the Pella area are familiar with still other reminders of the town's ethnic heritage, such as its summertime fair or *kermis*, and the December visit of *Sin-*

terklaas (who arrives aboard his ship from Spain and then rides his steed through town, dispensing sweets to well-behaved children and switches to the naughty).[4]

Vestiges of the Bilingual Heritage

Even the visitor to Pella who knows no Dutch may suspect that a foreign language has left its impact on this community's spoken English.[5] The careful listener might, for example, overhear individual Dutch words that are part of everyday parlance such as *vies* 'filthy; squeamish, fussy (about something that is dirty or messy)', *flauw* 'lethargic; vapid', *benauwd* 'anxious', *rommel* 'junk', or *knoeien* [around] 'to mess around, mess (or botch) up'. One might even hear a local denizen *brom* 'make noise; grumble' about someone who took too many *slokjes* 'gulps (of strong drink)' at a recent social event.

More likely is an encounter with interjections and short utterances in English so familiar to the local speaker that he no longer considers them to be nonstandard English (if indeed he ever did). Like Dutch *zeg*, exclamatory *say* may come at the end of a sentence: "those were pretty good results, *say!*" An unexpected statement (e.g., "I've not seen our friend since she returned home from vacation") may prompt a response such as "oh *so?*" or "oh *not?*"; as in Dutch, it is an affirming or negating adverb ("o *zo?*" "o *niet?*"), rather than an emphatic auxiliary verb ("Oh *have*n't you [or: *did*n't you] yet?"), which signals the conversation-partner's surprise.

Another adverb whose use in local English may appear unusual to the monolingual visitor is *yet*. Although the word seems redundant alongside *too* in utterances such as "She's got to do it *too yet*," it is merely functioning as a direct translation of Dutch *nog* 'yet, still, besides' ("Ze moet het ook nog doen"), where *nog* is not felt in any way to be extraneous or superfluous. Equally popular in the local lexicon is the adverbial particle *once*, which, like Dutch *eens* (from *een* 'one'), may lend the emphatic sense of *just* or *simply* to the verb of the sentence. The statement "I'd like to try it *once*" (cf. Dutch "ik zou het *eens* willen proberen") might best be understood in Pella as meaning "I'd *just* like to try that (once)." In combination with *too* and *yet*, *once* can contribute to such unforgetable utterances as "Would you like to lend a hand once too yet?" ("Wil je ook nog eens meehelpen?").

Prepositions (and adverbs derived from prepositions) also appear in usage patterns that may strike the noninitiate as unusual, if not downright foreign. When a fast-food restaurant recently opened in Pella, it was commonly reported among bargain-seekers that coffee was (only!) ten cents *by* (i.e., *at*) Hardee's (cf. "Koffie kost maar tien cent *bij* Hardee's"). One informant's wife reports that she can always recognize a certain party when he calls on the phone to speak with her husband. The voice is not so much the tip-off as the fact that the caller invariably asks whether the husband is *close by*, which the wife interprets as a blending of *close at hand* and *nearby* in attempting to translate Dutch *kort bij*.

Locals understand, of course, that the question "Are you going *with?*" really asks whether one is coming *along* ("Ga je *mee?*"). *Putting an egg through* something is not as messy a job as it sounds: it merely means blending the egg into the other ingredients of a batter ("Men klopt [er] een ei door"). Even as basic an event as water passing beneath a bridge may be expressed differently here, where the water is said by some (including at least a few primarily Anglophone residents!) to run *under through* the bridge, or *under* the bridge *through* (cf. "het water gaat [er] *onder door*"). Occasionally, one finds the preposition *with* used in a manner typical for Dutch, but unknown in English. When a non–Dutch-speaking friend wished to report that she and her husband had managed to spend some time together by themselves, she noted: "[my husband] and I went [on vacation] *with* just the two of us." This was one of the fairly rare, but by no means unparalleled, vestiges of a somewhat too literal translation of *met* in a sentence such as "we gingen met ons tweeën."

Attentive listeners will note that one *goes* (rather than *comes*) along with friends on a trip (cf. "*Ga* je mee?" cited above). A verb even more consistently influenced by Dutch models is *bring*, which, like Dutch *brengen*, can mean either 'bring' or 'take'. When I asked my strictly Anglophone (but 100 percent ethnically Dutch) neighbor whether she or her husband could give me a ride to the garage where my own car was being serviced, she cheerfully responded that her husband would be home from work in a few minutes and could "*bring* [me] uptown ("Hij kan je in de stad *brengen*").

Relatively few nouns appear to have been inspired by Dutch models, and those that have are easily identified as the legacy of Dutch life and culture. Older persons, for instance, may refer to December 31 as *Old Year Evening,* a direct translation of Dutch *oudejaarsavond.* One noun, however, has been used so frequently by persons of all ages that even the children of purely Anglophone families with no Dutch ties whatsoever pick it up at an early age. *Coffeetime* (Dutch *koffietijd*) has become the local term de rigeur for snacktime, and even for the snack food itself. Hence, a sitter might ask a parent what the children are supposed to have for coffeetime, without suggesting in any way that the youngsters be provided with something stronger than punch and cookies. Similarly, club notices often include the information that a potluck coffeetime will follow the business meeting.

One of the most ostensibly enjoyed by-products of Dutch and English in contact is "Yankee Dutch." First popularized in a series of publications now out of print and much sought by collectors, texts in this peculiar hybrid blend of forms from the two languages are often read at festive occasions such as wedding anniversaries and family reunions. When the late C. C. Buerkens featured a selection of Yankee Dutch in his folklore and folklife column for the local newspaper, he found himself besieged by requests from a readership eager to have more. The only solution, of course, was to offer the public what it wanted.[6]

Characteristic of Yankee Dutch are a number of puns based on words from the two languages that are homonymic, or at least are spelled similarly, but have different meanings in Dutch and English. Hence, there is nothing very jovial about *glad* streets in January (cf. Dutch *glad* 'slick'), nor is there anything particularly vulgar about a man *spitting* in his garden (cf. Dutch *omspitten* 'to turn over [earth] with a spade'). My all-time favorite came from a secretary who noted my barely surreptitious attempts to indulge my sweet tooth with candy filched from her desk, and commented with double entendre: "My, Professor, you certainly are a snoopy eater!" (cf. Dutch *snoep* 'sweets').

While Dutch immigrants in some parts of the United States may have tried to obscure or even obliterate the vestige of national origin left by a family name, relatively few such attempts have been made in Pella. Elsewhere, sensitive Dutchmen may have preferred a name like Young over Naaktgeboren ('born naked'—possibly a name originally adopted in grass-roots defiance of the Napoleonic Code, which mandated a surname for all); in Pella the name lives on and occasions gentle kidding, but, as far as I am able to tell, neither disdain of the meaning nor complaints about its pronunciation.[7] Similarly, no attempt was made to Americanize Niemantsverdriet, the translation of which ('nobody's sorrow') requires the same sort of euphemistic paraphrasing as Naaktgeboren.

Many a name is pronounced as it might be by a Dutchman: Vroom rhymes with Rome, Huizer with miser, and the syllables of Steenhoek rhyme with Wayne and Luke. Occasionally, a distinctly regional pronunciation prevails: Ver Dught, as in some northern Dutch dialects, is pronounced with [f] as its penultimate consonant. When a name change does occur, a Dutch form is often replaced by the English cognate. Hence, at one point some members of the originally Huguenot Le Cocq family took on the near-homonymic Dutch form De Kok ('the cook'), which in one American branch of the kinship appears "in translation" as De Cook. In other instances, the English homonym is good enough, even if the name's original meaning is thereby obscured. Slijkoord 'muddy place,' which is still seen on some older Pella tombstones in the Dutch form, has undergone a change of spelling and is now familiar to local residents as Slycord. Humor is often derived from familiar-sounding elements of names. Initiates will instantly understand a reference to "the maws and the straws" not as an allusion to mothers and animal bedding, but rather to persons of Frisian origin, whose family names frequently end in -ma (Jaarsma, Hoeksema) and -stra (Tuinstra, Klimstra). Needless to say, both intentionally and unwittingly false folk etymologies of names creep in, such as 'house in the field' for Heusinkveld (actually, 'nobleman's field') or 'hog hills' for Hoksbergen ('rounded hills'). Scholarly investigators confronted by such explanations from well-meaning but insistent informants often need to draw upon diplomatic, as well as analytical, skills.

Though nowadays younger members of the community seldom receive distinctly Dutch first names, such forms are often a source of pride among older residents. A few have adopted a more "American" name, (e.g., Steve for Stoffel [Christoffel]), but for the most part older informants beam with satisfaction at being allowed to reveal their "real" names. Some given names are part of a long family tradition, and the namesake may well be prepared to list all the relatives for several generations who have shared the name. (One extremely fluent informant, who has never been in the Netherlands, considers her relationship to a Dutch cousin with whom she regularly corresponds to be especially close by virtue of a shared baptismal name.) Other families appear to have made a fairly consistent practice of having their children "christened Dutch" (i.e., giving one form for the official record [Nelly, Tudor], and another to be used at the baptismal ceremony [Neeltje, Tuinis]). Some did not even go to that much trouble, and Gertje or Gradus simply had to serve as the given name for all occasions. If anything, it is the American who does not understand the name, rather than the Dutchman with the puzzling form, who is seen as laughable. Although the male (characteristically Frisian) name Oene was eventually changed by one immigrant, it was only done so after the bearer and his wife complained bitterly that the benighted local residents had misunderstood it for Anna ("daar hebben ze Anna van gemaakt").

Even in totally Anglophone circles of modern-day Pella, there is a striking propensity for the use of nicknames, a trend that appears to have antecedants in earlier times. In totally independent and spontaneous retellings of local lore, a number of interviewees volunteered the name of the town's legendary tramp, whose surname, Kruiter, seems to have served at one point as a synonym for *vagrant*; on the other end of the social spectrum, a certain individual had achieved sufficient prosperity to be seen as the prototype of financial success. One account, which may indeed be apocryphal, but nevertheless reflects local perceptions of what might plausibly have taken place, tells of children coming up to the local tycoon to ask him who he was. Showing real—or perhaps feigned—surprise at the question, the gentleman informed his young audience that he was none other than *de rijke De Wild* '(Mr.) De Wild the wealthy'. Perhaps the most frequently recalled nickname from earlier times was *Pruikje*, 'little wig'; evidently the proprietor of a certain local general store was among the first to introduce the use of a toupee, an item that attracted attention both for its novelty and for the wearer's much-attested talent for letting it fall into foodstuffs.

From the beginning, Pella has been not only Dutch (the telephone directory still devotes more than one fourth of its space to names beginning with the typically Dutch prefixes *De, Van,* and their variations); it is also conspicuously Christian, supporting close to twenty churches, about half of which are in some way allied with the Calvinist tradition. Several of these institutions, like individual members of the community, often bore a Dutch nickname. The church founded by H. P. Scholte (and now represented only by a replica in the local Historical Village) continues on occasion to be referred to as *de oude vierde kerk* 'the old fourth church'; older residents respond to *de hanekerk* 'the rooster church' as the name given to a building whose roof was once topped by a weathercock; and the local Darbyite congregation is still erroneously referred to by some as *de doodslapers* even though the sect known locally as the Soul Sleepers have not occupied the Darbyites' building for many years.[8] Children know by an early age whether or not they will bear the designation "offy," a term derived from *afgescheiden* 'separated' and first used to describe religious secessionists such as Scholte, and later in a derisive manner to identify members of the Christian Reformed Church, which split with the Reformed Church in America.

Sociolinguistic Investigation in Pella: Selection of Sources

IN at least a few limited circles, the use of Dutch as a salient characteristic of local community life will continue until some point in the early twenty-first century. If the language survives over a longer period, it will no doubt do so as the second language of those few who have taken pains to acquire it in a classroom setting, and only vestigially as the naturally acquired and transmitted language whose use is reported here.

Because this study focuses on the language as it has developed and been used locally, contrasts between local and supraregional "standard" Dutch (ABN or *algemeen beschaafd Nederlands*) are made only where doing so will clarify a point in the evolution of Pella Dutch, and never as a means of evaluating the relative "correctness" (or lack thereof) in the language of local residents.

I began collecting notes on Pella Dutch in the summer of 1976. By 1980, I was aware of some 250 persons who might qualify as potential sources for my research: individuals who had acquired functional fluency in Dutch principally in the Pella area (and at any rate, not in the Netherlands!), who enjoyed no formal schooling in the language until it had been acquired at a functional level, and who still continue to use Dutch with at least modest regularity in certain social situations.

About this time, new reportings of speaker-sources began to wane drastically. A sharing of my information with knowledgeable members of the community confirmed what I strongly suspected: for all practical purposes, the extent (and, in large part, even the exact membership) of the speaker pool had been determined.

With the appearance in 1981 of Nancy C. Dorian's

classic work on language obsolscence, *Language Death*, I decided to adopt a series of questionnaires of the sort presented in that study as a means of lending an organizational framework to my own work.[9] I was gratified when both Prof. Dorian and University of Wales' Prof. E. Glyn Lewis (on whose models some of Dorian's questionnaires are based) encouraged me to develop a survey mechanism appropriate for use in Pella. (See Appendix A.) At this point no advice was more pertinent than Dorian's: to use the questionnaires as a basis for determining areas requiring further attention, but to rely in the final instance on the experience gained by prolonged face-to-face contact with local speakers.[10]

The desirability of such a study rested on several points. Iowa is rich in ethnic communities, a few of which have been studied by linguists (James Dow, for instance, had provided a useful survey of German-speaking communities in Iowa, and Lawrence Rettig had produced several useful studies of Amana German). Nevertheless, the state has received only passing mention in such anthological works on language maintenance and language shift in the Midwest as the otherwise excellent collection of essays *Languages in Conflict:Linguistic Acculturation on the Great Plains*, edited by Paul Schach.[11] It is hoped that the present work will call attention to one of Iowa's bilingual communities, and perhaps prompt further sociolinguistic research elsewhere in the state.

Several problems arose in the specific selection of sources. First of all, a number of potential subjects for my survey proved to be ineligible for inclusion in the study. Some, as I learned upon closer contact, were immigrants from the Netherlands who arrived in the community already fluent in Dutch (and hence were really speakers of a form of the language for which scholarly studies abound, rather than users of the uniquely local idiom represented by the circle of speakers whom I sought); others spoke not

Dutch but Frisian, a language whose use in Pella certainly merits investigation, but falls outside the scope of this study; and a small number had indeed learned Dutch in Pella, but had long since ceased to use the language. Still others were prevented by health or other considerations from working with me; a number politely declined to be part of an investigative project; and a few had passed away before contact was possible. Between 1981 and 1982, I had identified a pool of some 200–250 potential sources, many of whom would not, unfortunately, be in a position to offer more than a brief interview.

At this point I became interested in the work by dialectologists who, faced at times with the necessity of working with limited numbers of speakers, had developed techniques for selection of a representative "community profile."[12] Sharing a working list of sources with members of the community whom I trusted to evaluate my profile of respondents, I arrived at a sampling of the speaker pool that, in the opinion of those who intimately know Pella's overall Dutch-speaking population, is typical (in terms of age, sex, residence patterns, educational level, work experience, and religious preference) for the group under study. While every attempt was made to keep the speaker-sample representative, it was nevertheless decided that older informants should be approached with particular dispatch.

In the end, over sixty persons completed the questionnaire, though several returns could not be tabulated, and the respondent data that follows, if not otherwise noted, is based on sixty reasonably complete survey returns. A handful of individuals gave long, narrative answers, which did not adhere strictly to the format of the questionnaire, and several others answered only a very few isolated questions; both types of response were kept on file, but were not tabulated. While there was a fairly high rate of nonresponse to any given question, the sporadic offerings of "chronic nonresponders" are not included in the statistical data of this section.

Of the slighty more than sixty persons who agreed to participate in the questionnaire process, forty-four granted a follow-up interview, which was usually taped. I worked closely with twelve additional individuals who declined to complete the questionnaire, but allowed me to interview them in sessions that varied considerably in length and degree of formality. Some had no objection to my recording the interview or taking extensive notes; others preferred simply to give brief answers to specific questions. In addition to these individuals, thirteen persons were interviewed by Gail Vande Bunte-De Somer as part of a Senior Honors project at Central College, completed under my supervision in 1980; three others were interviewed at my request by research assistant Jayne Gaunt; further data on lexical preference was gathered by Garry Davis from six otherwise untapped sources. Finally, I have engaged in some form of extended conversation with or observed spontaneous socializing by close to sixty other speakers of Pella Dutch.

As modest as the number of respondents may seem for a study based on the use of a survey mechanism, several points must be mentioned. First, by the time the research was completed (for the most part, near the end of the 1984-1985 academic year), I had been in one form of contact or another with close to 150 speakers. This represents nearly 75 percent of those eligible for inclusion in the study, and an even greater percentage of those who were in fact both willing and able to participate.

Based on my contact with this larger circle of individuals, I feel confident not only that the sampling of completed questionnaire respondents is representative of the larger community of speakers, but indeed that virtually every member of my broader circle of contacts was utilized in the manner (as a questionnaire respondent, interview subject, regular conversation partner, etc.) that was most appropriate and feasible under prevailing circumstances. Furthermore, I came to know my sources well enough to be able to judge in many an instance whether special weight or credence should (or should not) be given to a particular statement or opinion.

Finally, and perhaps best as an aside, it might be noted that while many forms of sociolinguistic inquiry rely upon information gained from larger numbers of survey participants, studies of obsolescent languages often deal, perforce, with a much smaller corpus of response data. For the generational strata roughly corresponding to the ages of most speakers of Pella Dutch, for instance, Dorian worked with a circle of some forty individuals.

Questionnaire Respondents as Representatives of the Speaker Pool

SOME 40 percent of the sixty speakers who responded to the questionnaire were born in Pella, with another 20 percent coming from adjacent communities in Marion county; 10 percent were born in neighboring Mahaska County, and 7 percent in adjoining Jasper County; 8 percent were born in other parts of Iowa, primarily Sioux and Lyon counties.[13] Of the remaining 15 percent, a handful were born in the Netherlands and moved to Pella at a very early age, were born elsewhere overseas (one as the child of missionaries in Japan), or were born in other ethnic Dutch communities in this country.

Approximately 70 percent of these speakers have

lived primarily in Pella throughout their lives, and an additional 10 percent live in surrounding communities. Less than one-third of the speakers have spent significant time outside Pella (frequently in other ethnic Dutch communities in Iowa), and these persons have invariably returned to Pella to maintain family ties, to secure a job with a local employer, or to retire in the community. It would appear, on the basis of my own observation, that the relative fluency of those who returned depended less on the length or brevity of absence from the community than on the personal inclination of a given speaker to reenter (or even to reestablish) circles of fellow speakers of Pella Dutch.

The speaker population is an aging one. (I have involuntarily acquired the habit of scanning the local newspaper for names of informants in the announcements of golden wedding anniversaries and in obituary notices.) Of the questionnaire respondents, only one identified himself as being between 30 and 40 years old; a mere three (or 5 percent) were in the 40- to 50-year old bracket. Twenty percent are between 50 and 60; 22 percent between 60 and 70; 28 percent between 70 and 80; and 17 percent 80 or over. While a few informants declined to give their age, various indicators place them in the 60- to 70-year-old range. Though primarily an older informant pool, the distribution by sex is approximately that of the general population for all ages: 52 percent female and 48 percent male.

The largest occupational classes represented are: farming (12 percent), education (12 percent), skilled labor (12 percent), housekeeping (10 percent), and services (8 percent). Fifty-two percent claim no special schooling, while 31 percent have attained at least one higher degree. The remaining informants enjoyed either specific vocational training or some other form of preparation for their present work. Only a handful have appreciable formal training in a foreign language, and those who have studied Dutch typically did so as adults.

While a number of respondents (13 percent) declined or were unable to give specific information on when their families immigrated to the United States, the majority (58 percent) were able to pinpoint the years of initial immigration by the ancestor who first arrived in Pella from the Netherlands (Table 1.1). All claimed some Dutch ancestry; for 87 percent, all four grandparents were of Dutch extraction; 57 percent noted that all four grandparents were in fact born in the Netherlands; another 13 percent claimed that at least two of the grandparents were natives of the Low Countries. For 40 percent of the informants, it was the grandparents who first migrated to this country, for another 23 percent the great-grandparents, and for only 17 percent the parents.

Table 1.1.   Decades of initial migration

Decade	Percent
1840	5
1850	15
1860	3
1870	15
1880	3
1890	7
1900–1920	8
after 1920	3

The Pella Historical Society is currently compiling a collection of family histories volunteered by local residents (who alone will be responsible for the content and accuracy of the articles submitted). While the work may at times require verification of detail, it will nevertheless provide an invaluable basis for investigation of immigration to the community.

Almost two-thirds (63 percent) of the respondents or their families have visited the Netherlands; 28 percent have done so on more than one occasion or for an extended period. The most frequently cited reason for travel

(54 percent of those going abroad) was to maintain family ties and/or to do genealogical research.

A full 80 percent of the respondents are able to identify the family's province(s) of origin; of these, close to 75 percent point to Gelderland as the family's homeland, 14 percent Friesland, and only a handful claim other provinces, notably South Holland and Utrecht.[14] About half of those able to identify the province(s) of origin maintain ongoing contacts in those areas. This is even more likely to be the case if the family originated in the villages of Gelderland. Of the approximately 30 percent of all speakers who make regular contact with persons in the ancestral home territory, over 60 percent do so with cousins. An almost formulaic account was given by those speakers who had been exhorted (or whose parents had been exhorted) by a grandparent not to allow family ties to lapse. The charge is taken seriously, and more than one individual bemoaned the fact that coming generations possess neither the interest nor linguistic facility necessary for continued contact. Although relatively few respondents identified themselves as fluent writers, 32 percent (or 51 percent, adjusted for nonresponses on this item of the questionnaire) maintain some form of correspondence with family or close personal friends in the Netherlands.

Not surprisingly, respondents tended to identify themselves as ethnically Dutch, though perhaps not so intensely as one might expect: 55 percent classed themselves as "strongly" and 28 percent as "moderately" ethnic Dutch; 12 percent, however, thought of themselves as only "remotely" ethnically Dutch, and (even though no such specific option was offered on the questionnaire) 5 percent chose to make special note of the fact that they either considered themselves not to be ethnically Dutch, or would accept the designation only with certain qualifications.[15]

Language Background

ONLY one respondent, an individual who learned the language primarily from a hired hand, could recall no Dutch having been spoken at home; 90 percent recall frequent (and another 8 percent occasional) exposure to Dutch in the family circle. The question as to just when Dutch was spoken at home elicited a variety of responses, though several patterns emerged. A mere 12 percent of those polled recall Dutch as the only language spoken at home, though for 17 percent of the respondents it was the only language used before entering school. Apart from special occasions, Dutch appears generally to have been used with ever decreasing frequency after the 1950s.

Forty percent of those who completed the questionnaire grew up in families where all members spoke Dutch; 66 percent recall parents (and 42 percent their siblings) as frequent speakers. Virtually all who recall specific members of the family teaching them Dutch identify a parent as the teacher. (See Part Three for a discussion of the influence of speakers from outside the family circle.) Not one speaker identified siblings per se as teachers of Dutch (though often enough siblings were cited as major sources of instruction in English). Once Dutch was acquired, it tended to be spoken almost 80 percent of the time with the parents or in the presence of the parents. (It is also interesting to note that it is always the parents—or the amorphous "entire family," and never siblings as such— who are identified as the persons who *encouraged* the informant to use Dutch.) Indeed, only 27 percent recall actually being part of conversations in Dutch with *all* family members present. This, coupled with the fact that only 32 percent of the informants have made any attempt to teach

Dutch to their children (and the younger the informant, the less the likelihood of such an attempt), would lead even the most optimistic to think of Pella Dutch as a language whose heyday is past.

Only a handful of speakers had the benefit of formal training in Dutch.[16] Three questionnaire respondents spent appreciable time in the Netherlands, and another enjoyed training in the language at the Christian School in nearby Peoria, Iowa. Five returned to school as adults, revitalizing their language skills by taking courses in Dutch at Central College. The only pattern to emerge with any frequency, however, was that of language instruction in cathechism class, which frequently consisted not only of doctrine, but also (indeed, some say primarily) in learning to read the key Biblical and dogmatic texts in Dutch, and in memorizing the rhymed Psalms in Dutch *(de berijmde psalmen)*.

About three-quarters (73 percent) of the respondents recall having once attended church services in Dutch, and insofar as memory served them, approximately half of all who completed the questionnaire remember their own use of Dutch while at church. (Both major branches of the Dutch-American Calvinist tradition, the Reformed Church in America and the Christian Reformed Church, are represented in the informant pool, with Christian Reformed respondents constituting a slight majority among survey participants.) Although only a few individuals responded with specific details to questions asking just where and when these Dutch-language church services were held, a clear pattern emerged from follow-up interviews. Apart from a few churches (such as Pella's Second Reformed Church) that have always held services in English, Dutch was the common language of worship up to World War I; between the World Wars, Dutch was used at certain times, such as during the afternoon service or on a fortnightly basis; and by the 1940s and 1950s, the use of Dutch in church services was in irreversible decline. It is interesting to note, however, that the recollection of a service being held in Dutch remains a particularly vivid memory for many of the younger speakers who were able to experience such an event.

Roughly one-half of the questionnaire respondents use Dutch on the job, or did so when last employed. In this context, it is most frequently spoken with fellow workers, though about one-third of those who speak the language on the job do (or did) so with customers. (Use of Dutch at the place of work need not be exclusively with humans; more than one farmer confided that contact with ill-tempered animals helps him to maintain an active vocabulary of terms not typically found in a beginner's lexicon of the language.) The only clubs or societies where Dutch appears to have been used with any frequency, though not necessarily as the group's official language, were church consistory (reported by 22 percent of the informants), church aid societies (reported by 15 percent) and, in earlier years, the various committees connected with Tulip Time or other ethnic celebrations (reported by 8 percent). Continued use of the language in such circles today is sporadic and dictated strictly by individual preference. Among other occasions that might prompt the use of Dutch today, three stand out: wedding anniversaries (where readings of Yankee Dutch, as discussed earlier, are common); funerals (especially of older persons); and family reunions, where use of the language may serve as an open affirmation of a common heritage.[17]

General Patterns of Language Use

MUCH of the best statistical information on language use in Pella comes from responses to questionnaire inquiries about the frequency with which one tends to use Dutch with certain speaker partners. The data in Table 1.2 and in the subsequent tables give percentages of response (and then the absolute number of responses) to various questionnaire items. As an aside I might note that I specifically asked participants to give information about *current* speaking patterns. It became clear, however, that many speakers were lured by the opportunity to comment on the situation of former years, and generally speaking, I allowed them to do so, while making note of what was happening. To give but one concrete example, I was inclined, after an initial failure to find young children using even barbarized Dutch, to eliminate the questions dealing with the use of Dutch on the playground, in school, etc. By that point, however, I had received such a spontaneous outpouring of information on the former use (or nonuse) of Dutch in these contexts that I decided to retain the questions as a stimulus to the sharing of valuable recollections. (I have therefore noted those items where respondents answered in a historical context.) It should also be noted that information on the use of Dutch in the family circle is, for the most part, current; insights into language use in the childhood family circle were gained from other parts of the questionnaire.

Although several points illustrated in Table 1.2 will be discussed in greater detail in later sections, a few items merit immediate attention. Older speaker partners are more likely to prompt a code-switch to Dutch than are younger ones; Dutch is more frequently used with grandparents than with parents, and more frequently with

Table 1.2. Frequency of using Dutch with other speakers

Speaker	Always	Usually	Often	Sometimes	Never	Does not apply	No response
Parents	21.7% (13)[a]	8.3% (5)	8.3% (5)	20.0% (12)	6.7% (4)	16.7% (10)	18.3% (11)
Grandparents	21.7 (13)	. . .	. . .	11.7 (7)	3.3 (2)	38.3 (23)	25.0 (15)
Spouse daily	3.3 (2)	1.7 (1)	13.3 (8)	33.3 (20)	21.7 (13)	10.0 (6)	16.7 (10)
Spouse when angry	1.7 (1)	1.7 (1)	3.3 (2)	8.3 (5)	35.0 (21)	16.7 (10)	33.3 (20)
Spouse when children are present	. . .	3.3 (2)	11.7 (7)	16.7 (10)	28.3 (17)	15.0 (9)	25.0 (15)
Children	. . .	1.7 (1)	1.7 (1)	23.3 (14)	31.7 (19)	13.3 (8)	28.3 (17)
Children when angry	1.7 (1)	. . .	1.7 (1)	11.7 (7)	40.7 (24)	15.0 (9)	30.0 (18)
In-laws	6.7 (4)	5.0 (3)	6.7 (4)	25.0 (15)	21.7 (13)	11.7 (7)	23.3 (14)
Older siblings	1.7 (1)	6.7 (4)	10.0 (6)	25.0 (15)	23.3 (14)	6.7 (4)	26.7 (16)
Younger siblings	. . .	. . .	8.3 (5)	21.7 (13)	20.0 (12)	16.7 (10)	33.3 (20)
Close relatives	1.7 (1)	1.7 (1)	15.0 (9)	41.7 (25)	13.3 (8)	1.7 (1)	25.0 (15)
Classmates on playground[b]	1.7 (1)	5.0 (3)	5.0 (3)	8.3 (5)	11.7 (7)	30.0 (18)	38.3 (23)
Classmates in school[b]	. . .	. . .	6.7 (4)	13.3 (8)	20.0 (12)	25.0 (15)	35.0 (21)
Best friend, in public	. . .	. . .	3.3 (2)	51.7 (31)	15.0 (9)	. . .	30.0 (18)
Best friend, in private	. . .	. . .	13.3 (8)	46.7 (28)	16.7 (10)	. . .	23.3 (14)
Minister	. . .	1.7 (1)	1.7 (1)	16.7 (10)	35.0 (21)	10.0 (6)	35.0 (21)
At work with boss	. . .	. . .	. . .	3.3 (2)	18.3 (11)	41.7 (25)	36.7 (22)
At work with employee(s)	. . .	. . .	1.7 (1)	21.7 (13)	10.0 (6)	33.3 (20)	33.3 (20)
Acquaintances	. . .	. . .	5.0 (3)	51.7 (31)	10.0 (6)	8.3 (5)	25.0 (15)
Shopping, with sales persons	. . .	. . .	. . .	28.3 (17)	30.0 (18)	10.0 (6)	31.7 (19)
At religious services	. . .	. . .	. . .	21.7 (13)	33.3 (20)	10.0 (6)	30.0 (21)

Table 1.2. *(Continued)*

Speaker	Always	Usually	Often	Sometimes	Never	Does not apply	No response
With boyfriend/ girlfriend in public[b]	...	...	...	...	6.7 (4)	51.7 (31)	41.7 (25)
With boyfriend/ girlfriend in private[b]	...	...	...	...	13.3 (8)	46.7 (28)	40.0 (24)
Doctor	...	...	...	21.7 (13)	31.7 (19)	8.3 (5)	38.3 (23)
Teacher[b]	...	...	...	5.0 (3)	35.0 (21)	23.3 (14)	36.7 (22)
Neighbors	...	...	1.7 (1)	53.3 (32)	16.7 (10)	6.7 (4)	21.7 (13)
Household pets	...	3.3 (2)	8.3 (5)	6.7 (4)	20.0 (12)	18.3 (11)	43.3 (26)

[a]Number of respondents.
[b]Respondents answered in a historical context.

parents or parents-in-law than with children; older siblings are somewhat more probable Dutch speaker partners than are younger siblings. These facts alone suggest that we are dealing with an obsolescent language, and other indicators also lead us to the same conclusion. A fair number of respondents and other sources reported that they speak Dutch daily with their spouses, for instance, yet a far smaller number speak Dutch with the spouse when children are present, or with the children themselves. In a nutshell, the cross-generational continuity of language use is eroding.

It is also noteworthy that Dutch is used less with either spouse or children if the speaker is angry. Comments from follow-up interviews seem to indicate that the language has indeed lost some of its vitality as a carrier of emotionally charged utterances, whether of anger, joy, frustration, or satisfaction. This situation can hardly bode well for the future of Dutch in Pella.

Tempering and qualifying some of these conclusions

are data gathered on use of Dutch for various activities requiring language use (Table 1.3).

Evidently, any loss of emotional vigor in Pella Dutch does not necessarily mean that residents of Pella are there-

Table 1.3. *Frequency Dutch is used in various language-intensive activities*

Activity	Always	Usually	Often	Sometimes	Never	Does not apply	No response
Read books	...	1.7% (1)[a]	8.3% (5)	40.0% (24)	31.7% (19)	1.7% (1)	16.7% (10)
Read newspapers	...	3.3 (2)	...	23.3 (14)	40.0 (24)	6.7 (4)	26.7 (16)
Read Bible/Psalms	1.7 (1)	5.0 (3)	3.3 (2)	38.3 (23)	30.0 (18)	...	21.6 (13)
Hear sermons	...	3.3 (2)	1.7 (1)	23.3 (14)	46.7 (28)	...	25.0 (15)
Correspond	1.7 (1)	3.3 (2)	1.7 (1)	25.0 (15)	48.3 (29)	...	20.0 (12)
Speak with fellow workers	...	1.7 (1)	5.0 (3)	26.7 (16)	15.0 (9)	28.3 (17)	23.3 (14)
Pray	1.7 (1)	1.7 (1)	1.7 (1)	15.0 (9)	55.0 (33)	...	25.0 (15)
Dream	...	1.7 (1)	...	1.7 (1)	51.7 (31)	3.3 (2)	41.7 (25)
Curse	1.7 (1)	5.0 (3)	...	23.3 (14)	40.0 (24)	5.0 (3)	25.0 (15)
Count	1.7 (1)	1.7 (1)	8.3 (5)	33.3 (20)	33.3 (20)	...	21.7 (13)
Make telephone calls	...	1.7 (1)	5.0 (3)	38.3 (23)	33.3 (20)	...	21.7 (13)
Speak with persons from elsewhere in U.S.	...	1.7 (1)	...	26.7 (16)	38.3 (23)	5.0 (3)	28.3 (17)
Discuss local affairs	...	1.7 (1)	...	15.0 (9)	45.0 (27)	6.7 (4)	31.7 (19)
Discuss national affairs	...	1.7 (1)	...	15.0 (9)	45.0 (27)	6.7 (4)	31.7 (19)
Discuss religion	...	3.3 (2)	...	30.0 (18)	36.7 (22)	1.7 (1)	28.3 (17)
Discuss finances	...	1.7 (1)	...	8.3 (5)	51.7 (31)	5.0 (3)	33.3 (20)
Discuss health	...	1.7 (1)	3.3 (2)	18.3 (11)	45.0 (27)	1.7 (1)	30.0 (18)

[a]Number of respondents.

fore unable to muster up strong epithets in the language of their forefathers. Though 25 percent of those polled did not answer the question, and another 45 percent maintained that they never curse in Dutch (or that the question simply does not apply!), a full 30 percent admit to using strong Dutch on occasion. In view of the number of persons who claim to read the Bible or Psalms in Dutch, and who say they discuss religion in Dutch, it is interesting to note that more respondents admitted to cursing in Dutch than to praying in Dutch. The meaning of this statistic is not entirely clear and certainly open to a variety of interpretations.

On the whole, the speakers who responded to the questionnaire are better, or at least more frequent, readers than they usually claim to be (a point touched upon elsewhere). Very few classify themselves as strong readers of Dutch, and yet the language activities involving the printed word rate rather high in comparison with other possible uses of the language. Subscribers and former subscribers to Dutch-language newspapers such as *De Wachter*, for instance, outnumber nonsubscribers by more than two to one. Similarly, few rate themselves fluent writers, and yet as seen before and noted once again in this data, there is an appreciable number of informants (albeit a minority) who correspond in Dutch.

The Dutch reading matter of Pella's current speaker is primarily religious, with few having ever read a novel in Dutch. Several noted that since the loss in the 1940s of Pella's Dutch-language newspaper, written and edited by local residents, there has not really been appropriate secular periodic reading material in *accessible* Dutch. Publications such as those of the Dutch International Society (formerly the Dutch Immigrant Society) are felt to be in language comprehensible primarily to immigrants and others familiar with the current speech of the Netherlands. Albeit at times archaic, it is the vocabulary and grammar of the Bible and of devotional literature (such as the popular *Hart en Leven*) with which most are comfortable.

The relatively common use of Dutch to converse with fellow workers and to make telephone calls indicates that it remains a language of socializing among persons who enjoy frequent and often informed contact with one another. It is noteworthy that Dutch is used considerably less frequently to discuss local or national affairs, finances, or health. The impression left during follow-up interviews was that recent Dutch immigrants to the United States have preferred to become Americanized (and hence Anglophones) as quickly as possible, and as a result there simply are no current and convenient sources of the specialized vocabulary needed by speakers of Pella Dutch in order to participate in more technically oriented conversations. When they do converse in Dutch with local speakers, immigrants have been observed sending out rather blatant signals that they do not feel Pella's speech reaches the standards of Dutch in the fatherland, thereby discouraging (whether intentionally or not) further use and development of the local idiom.

As an aside, a word deserves to be said about dreaming in Dutch. During one-to-one interviews, it became clear that many individuals simply did not know whether they dreamed in Dutch or in English. A small group, however, including about 10 percent who initially gave no response on the questionnaire, confided that dreaming in Dutch was prompted, although only on occasion, by the experience of sudden, intense contact with the language (e.g., upon receiving a visit from the Netherlands, or after reading Dutch books requiring a degree of concentration).

Further insight into patterns of language use is reflected in Table. 1.4. It would indeed seem that the language has lost some of its emotional valence if it is no longer the preferred language for recalling the memorable events of childhood, when Dutch was the major language

Table 1.4. Preference of Dutch for certain purposes

Purpose of language	Dutch preferred	English preferred	No marked preference	No response
Pass on proverbs, sayings	38.3%	25.0%	26.7%	10.0%
	(23)[a]	(15)	(16)	(6)
Plan a trip	1.7	81.7	5.0	11.7
	(1)	(49)	(3)	(7)
Recall childhood	13.3	55.0	20.0	8.3
	(8)	(33)	(12)	(7)
Talk to confidant	6.7	66.7	16.7	10.0
	(4)	(40)	(10)	(6)
Talk about news in paper	8.3	73.3	6.7	11.7
	(5)	(44)	(4)	(7)
Tell a joke	18.3	43.3	28.3	10.0
	(11)	(26)	(17)	(6)
Make a derogatory comment	21.7	40.0	23.3	15.0
	(13)	(24)	(14)	(9)
Greet a friend	15.0	48.3	28.3	8.3
	(9)	(29)	(17)	(5)
Greet a stranger	3.3	80.0	6.7	10.0
	(2)	(48)	(4)	(6)
Say something intimate	18.3	51.7	16.7	13.3
	(11)	(31)	(10)	(8)
Say something private in a crowd	56.7	26.7	10.0	6.7
	(34)	(16)	(6)	(4)

[a]Number of respondents.

for most respondents. It would also appear that speakers do not feel comfortable with highly specific vocabulary, such as is needed to plan a trip. As a language of light-hearted socializing, however, Dutch holds its own. On repeated occasions, it was noted that it is simply more fun to repeat a proverb or tell a joke if phrased in the language of the Low Countries.

It was striking how frequently and how utterly spontaneously respondents offered comments (both on the questionnaire and in subsequent interviews) on the vastly differing appropriateness of using Dutch as a secret code in which to make a derogatory comment, and as the language in which to say something private (but without malicious intent) in a public setting. Speakers are painfully aware that many a nonspeaker will suspect (on the basis of nonverbal clues) that Dutch is being used to make a derogatory comment. The nonspeaker may consequently suffer (or imagine suffering) the double insult of being defamed, and at that in a manner that allows no recourse to satisfactory self-vindication. The need to say something private, which may be of no concern whatsoever to a third party, however, (e.g., "my new shoes hurt") is considered a wonderful and perfectly appropriate occasion on which to use Dutch as an exclusionary code.

Awareness of and Attitudes toward Language Use

EXCLUDING disclaimers and qualifications (such as "I'm not really a language scholar, but . . ."), all respondents were able to recognize varying levels of fluency among their fellow speakers, and in general their appraisals were both accurate and fair. Ability to recognize another dialect, however, seemed to pose greater problems. About one-fourth of the individuals felt they could recognize a speaker of *Fries* (Frisian), which in fact is not a dialect of Dutch at all, but rather a separate minority language spoken principally in one province of the Netherlands. About the same number claim they can recognize a speaker whose dialect is that of Gelderland, and a few individual speakers maintain that they can identify one or more other regional speech patterns. As discussed in Part III, however, dialect remains an issue of interest to many speakers.

On the whole, participants in the questionnaire survey rated themselves as good or even excellent speakers, moderately competent readers, and poor writers; most are aware that the language they speak is nativelike in its spontaneity, and yet distinct from the Dutch spoken in the Netherlands. Those who are aware that they do not speak "standard" Dutch, however, are seldom able to pinpoint differences between their own Dutch and that of their linguistic cousins in the Low Countries, and are frequently unable to produce a "Holland Dutch" form on demand.[18]

Relatively few responses were given to questions concerning the perceived advantages of being able to speak Dutch: 7 percent felt that use of the language added a sense of warmth and closeness to family life; 10 percent felt it good to have someone in the church who could use the language with those (primarily older) members desiring it; 13 percent saw an advantage (albeit as much to the community as to specific individuals) in having speakers of Dutch who could be in direct linguistic contact with the roots of Pella's ethnic heritage. Even fewer respondents saw any disadvantage in speaking Dutch, though the less than 10 percent who did cite a negative side to bilingualism were outspoken in describing the resentment felt by nonspeakers excluded from the social interaction of those who are fluent in both languages.

When asked which reasons might be cited for learning Dutch, a variety of responses were given (Table 1.5). In a community where pragmatism and commercial success are highly prized, it was a bit surprising that the highest ratings went to essentially idealistic or even sentimental reasons: it is broadening to learn an additional language, and Dutch is a rich and beautifully expressive language. It is also worth noting that several respondents penned in notes on the questionnaire sheet stating that one might be able to understand Pella today, or even feel a part of the community, without knowing Dutch, but such was adamantly reported not to have been the case in earlier times.

Responses where spontaneous comparisons were made by a number of individuals between previous and current circumstances are noted in Table 1.5. Well over half of the persons who participated in a follow-up interview expressed the sentiment that one could get along just fine in Pella today as an English-speaking monolingual, but would have been a marked outsider, an "American" [*sic*], in former times.)

Should Dutch be preserved in Pella? About three-fourths (76.7 percent) of the survey participants (or 85.2 percent, adjusted for nonresponses to this question) feel that it should be, primarily to keep a sense of heritage

Table 1.5. Perceived benefits of knowing Dutch

Reason to learn Dutch	Very important	Important	Unimportant	No opinion	No response
It is broadening	46.7% (28)[a]	33.3% (20)	. . .	8.3% (5)	11.7% (7)
Enjoy Dutch music	10.0 (6)	31.7 (19)	20.0 (12)	16.7 (10)	21.7 (13)
It is rich and expressive	45.0 (27)	28.3 (17)	5.0 (3)	5.0 (3)	16.7 (10)
To understand Pella[b]	3.3 (2)	30.0 (18)	26.7 (16)	6.7 (4)	33.3 (20)
To feel part of the community[b]	5.0 (3)	33.3 (20)	25.0 (15)	8.3 (5)	26.7 (17)
To read books/ Bible	8.3 (5)	30.0 (18)	23.3 (14)	10.0 (6)	28.3 (17)
To have a secret language	8.3 (5)	26.7 (16)	36.7 (22)	6.7 (4)	21.7 (13)
To speak with friends/neighbors[b]	6.7 (4)	48.3 (29)	20.0 (12)	3.3 (2)	21.7 (13)
To understand programs	6.7 (4)	35.0 (21)	30.0 (18)	6.7 (4)	21.7 (13)
To speak with persons from elsewhere in U.S.	16.7 (10)	45.0 (27)	11.7 (7)	1.7 (1)	25.0 (15)
To participate in music/dance groups	11.7 (7)	26.7 (16)	15.0 (9)	13.3 (8)	33.3 (20)
It is beautiful to hear/speak	40.0 (24)	33.3 (20)	1.7 (1)	5.0 (3)	20.0 (12)

[a]Number of respondents.
[b]Respondents spontaneously compared previous and current circumstances.

alive. The schools (favored by 48.3 percent), community organizations (46.7 percent) and the family (36.7 percent) were seen as the proper places for language instruction. (Few respondents seemed aware that, at various times since the late 1950s, Pella Community Schools, Pella Christian Schools, and the Peoria Christian School had all offered Dutch as an elective enrichment course, and that each attempt was abandoned, after no more than two years, as demanding too much effort and resources for too little return.[19]) The 10 percent who favored the church as a center of language instruction were outnumbered almost two-to-one by those who opposed the idea (rather vehemently, in some cases). About one-fourth of the respondents feel that use of Dutch adds to family cohesiveness and serves to instill religious or moral values; each of these ideas was opposed by about 10 percent of the survey participants. About half feel that knowledge of Dutch is valuable in transmitting a sense of ethnic heritage, and only a single individual expressed the opinion that it is not.

The one situation felt to be serious enough to demand use of one language or the other is the funeral, where the presumed wishes of the deceased are honored. Slightly more than one-half (52 percent) of the respondents believe that strong pride in the Dutch heritage is likely to lead to language fluency, and vice versa. Less than 10 percent feel that there is no necessary connection between the two, and slightly more than 10 percent note that there might possibly be a connection between the two, but hesitate to make a blanket statement. Only a handful (about 5 percent in each instance) thought that they might be biased toward a political candidate or merchant who speaks Dutch.

About one-third of those surveyed had no opinion as to whether the person who is fluent in Dutch is somehow in closer contact with his religious roots; approximately one-third rejected the idea altogether, and roughly another one-third felt that the perception might be accurate in some instances or under certain circumstances.

Does speaking Dutch bring particular status or advantage? Though not expressed by all, the ironic idea cropped up in several interviews that, at the time of the oldest speakers' earliest recollections, knowledge of Dutch was simply expected; later, in the post—World War I trend toward embracing all things distinctively American, the language gradually fell into ever greater disuse, and its perceived value declined; today, when true bilingualism can no longer be presupposed, its value is once more, though ever so slowly, gaining both esteem and recognition.

PART TWO

The Culture

Photo by Les Sadler

Preparations for Tulip Time included street scrubbing, queuing up for imported tulip bulbs, and presenting light operettas on Dutch themes. In more recent years, Sinterklaas has introduced a distinctively Dutch element into Pella's annual calendar of celebrations.

Photo by Les Sadler

Evolving Attitudes toward
Language and Ethnicity

WHILE many of the following recollections, observations, and excerpts from the historical record might as easily appear in an ethnographic monograph or even in a work of popular history (rather than in a strictly linguistic study), no section of this book is more important to an understanding of how Pella's Dutch-Americans have tended over time to view their ethnicity and their language. Virtually every speaker stood poised to tell a tale of what it has meant to be Dutch and to be a speaker of the language, and as often as not, when individuals were not answering specific questions on language forms or use, they attempted to steer the conversation toward a sharing of just such recollections. I have tried here to present a distillation of these often poignant personal accounts as a complement to the primarily objective material of the other parts, and thereby offer an insight into how members of the speaker pool feel, at the most subjective level, about their heritage and about the language that until within their own lifetime was the chief vehicle by which that heritage was transmitted.

Eendracht Maakt Macht, or:
Divide and Be Conquered[1]

A T first glance, Pella appears to be a fairly homogeneous ethnic community. This initial impression of cohesiveness and ethnic solidarity is reinforced by the local residents' fairly precise understanding of just how far Dutch territory extends, and just where the "American" sphere of influence begins. (See Figure 2.1, where boundaries of "Dutch Territory" attempt at best to present a consensus of opinions, rather than fixed lines of demarcation.) Oskaloosa, seventeen miles to the southeast, is viewed as an American town made tolerable by a fairly large Dutch representation. New Sharon, about the same distance to the northeast, and Knoxville, a few miles closer than either of the other two and the Marion County seat, are frequently written off as being beyond the pale, despite visible Dutch constituencies. The small nearby communities of Peoria, Otley (where all five pupils and the teacher of a recently enrolled elementary class had names beginning with Van), and Leighton are accorded the status of "ours" (i.e., Dutch) not only on the basis of actual ethnic representation, but also on the relative loyalty of their residents to the Reformed or Christian Reformed Church.[2]

In former times, there were several additional tiny outposts, such as Bethel (or the Bethel-*buurt* [neighborhood]) north and west of Pella, and Olivet to the south between Tracy and Leighton, which were felt to be notably Dutch both in heritage and perception. Most such communities have lost their place on the map and can no longer be observed by an outside investigator, though it is interesting to note that an almost mythic memory lingers on in some circles of a time and a place characterized by

42

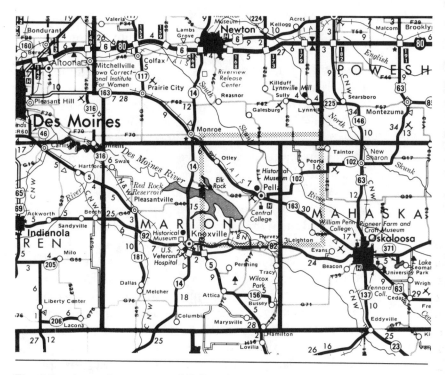

Fig. 2.1.   Approximate extent of Pella's "Dutch Territory"
(Reprinted, by permission, from the Iowa Department of Transportation.)

an unadulterated ethnic integrity that is being lost in Pella.

A closer view, however, allows us to see that the reported halcyon unity of earlier days was not altogether impervious to divisions of various sorts. It has been noted by several scholars that the Dutch who migrated to America tended not to come as individuals, but rather as part of transplanted communities. Hence, the Dutchman arriving in Pella was interested not merely in allying himself with compatriots from the homeland, but specifically with other persons from his province, if possible with those from his hometown, and wherever opportunity presented itself, with his own kinfolk.[3]

At least in the Pella area, homestead sites seem to

have been chosen with an eye toward finding environments similar to, or reminiscent of, familiar ones in the Netherlands. Hence, the Frisians gravitated toward the open prairie land northwest of Pella, immigrants from Gelderland sought out the rocky, hilly timberland south of town, and the relatively few Groningers settled in the Lake Prairie district with its opportunities for pasturing, garden farming, and nursery cultivation. Those who settled in town were more likely to have been from an urban background in the homeland.[4]

As a result, several local areas came to be known as the *buurt* or neighborhood of a particular regional group. In a world view that saw things relegated to their natural and proper places, residents of the *Frieze buurt* had their roots in Friesland, and the Herwijners of the *Herwijnse buurt* claimed family ties in the village of Herwijnen in Gelderland. Not too surprisingly, the flocking together of birds of a feather encouraged the development of various prejudicial stereotypes (e.g., "De Friezen zijn allemaal stijfkoppen" [All Frisians are stiff-headed] or "The folks from Gelderland are a contrary bunch"). Even more important for this study is the fact (documented in greater detail in Part III) that persons raised with others of the same regional background tended not merely to learn Dutch, but quite specifically the local dialect of their ancestors, and to transmit this, rather than the "standard language" or an amalgam influenced by the speech of the various provinces represented in Pella, to their own children.

Divisions also existed according to real or perceived social class structures. One source particularly willing to recount not only the events of his own youth, but also things heard from his father, gave the following account (by no means unique among the offerings of those interviewed). There were the "blue bloods . . . they carried a high stigma [*sic*] and there were ordinary Dutch, and each knew where he belonged." Certain areas, (e.g., the Lake Prairie district east of town) were known as "commoners' " turf. The residents of the *buurt* that was home to his own family were said to be incorrigably *verbasterd* 'degenerate, corrupt'. When his father realized the situation he had gotten himself into by seeking to live among his "own people," and that he could not readily associate with local residents from other parts of the homeland, he cursed the fate of being "locked into" a *buurt* whose land was not as productive as that of farmsteads elsewhere in the Pella area.

Negative manifestations notwithstanding, the Dutch tradition of regional and family particularism persisted well into the present century, eventually becoming institutionalized in the celebration of various annual picnics and reunions. There were clan picnics (even today, a summertime edition of the weekly *Pella Chronicle* may carry notices for a dozen or more such events), picnics for erstwhile schoolmates, and, of course, picnics for persons associated with a certain *buurt*. For some, the annual picnic featured an in-group talent show, and there are some proud Frisian-Americans who claim that their picnic was the forerunner of Tulip Time.[5] For those who might have cast their lot outside the Pella area, the picnic served as a sort of annual homecoming. The single picnic that seems to have received the most attention, however, and serves as the epitome par excellence of what the *buurt* came to stand for, is the well-nigh legendary Herwijnse picnic.

In 1930, the Herwijners (actual immigrants from Herwijnen in the Netherlands, descendents, relatives, and invited friends) held the first and largest of their picnics, in the heart of *buurt* country, on the wooded knolls of the Tunis and Uranus Van Dusseldorp farm (three miles south of town, east of the present Elevator Road). If front-page reports in *The Pella Press* may be given credence, fifteen hundred persons reached the site by noon, and by mid-afternoon a grand total of "fully three thousand" souls had assembled, some from as far away as Sioux County, Iowa and South Dakota.[6]

The program for the day included a morning report in Dutch, and an even more extensive afternoon address in English, by a Herwijner from nearby Oskaloosa who had just returned from a visit to the home village in the Netherlands, bringing back many collective and individual greetings. A poem was recited in Dutch on the theme of patriotism, with still further edification provided by a local minister (from the Baptist congregation, no less). Two ladies from prominent Herwijner families offered readings, and the sagacious Leendert Hackert, known for his "happy way of telling . . . stories . . . appreciated by everyone," and who for many years kept the Herwijner organization alive, recalled how he had fared on his last visit to the fatherland.[7] Group officers were elected, and it was decided to hold the picnic on the same site in the following year.

In addition to such features, there was much light-hearted amusement. The non-Dutch daughters of a local doctor gave their version of a wooden shoe dance. Asa Niemantsverdriet, who survived into his tenth decade in the 1980s and was to become one of the community's living links with the past, conducted an auction in the traditional Dutch manner, moving *down* to the bidder's price. There were ball games, a tug-of-war, sack races, and a grain-binding contest. Small wonder that *The Pella Press* declared the picnic "one of the jolliest meetings held in this community."[8]

For all that, it appears that Malice had entered Wonderland. Discontent was expressed with the organization and conduct of the picnic, and some of these grievances are remembered more than fifty years later. Dutchmen and Dutch-Americans from elsewhere who came to the picnic expecting to dance were disappointed by the stringent taboo that proscribes (as it still does in some circles of Pella society) such carnal forms of entertainment. Even more serious complaints centered around that item so dear to the heart of every true Dutchman: money.[9]

The Pella Press reported that those who did not bring a picnic basket "made a rush to the canteen which was conducted by the Porter Grove Aid Society, . . . and by the way the crowd devoured the stock in trade, it goes without saying that the ladies did a rushing business."[10] In this and subsequent years, suspicion and jealousy about money supposedly being made off the picnic produced rifts within the organization leading to relocation (to nearby Sully) and eventually, due to the inevitable forces of inertia, to a more modest celebration held in town at West Market Park and finally to total discontinuation of the event. Perhaps the reporter from *The Pella Press* suspected that such divisive forces simmered below the joyous surface when it was reported, in the middle of an otherwise upbeat article on "this best event of the year,. . . that no one was afraid of each other"—as though somehow that should be a newsworthy achievement![11]

Divisions according to regional origins and the bickering that may have arisen within and between the various constituent groups of the earlier community pale in comparison, however, with the cleavage over an even more basic issue, in which ethnic solidarity (or lack thereof) would be of paramount importance in determining the town's character.

Who Are "We" and Who Are "They"?

A LL evidence suggests that the leaders of the mid-nineteenth-century Dutch migrants to the American Midwest encouraged their followers to think of themselves as true citizens of the new homeland. Reverend Scholte did not fail to note with obvious delight that his brave little band left an impression of cleanliness, orderliness, and pious sincerity, reminiscent of the Pilgrims themselves, to those witnessing their arrival.[12] It was no doubt a reputation based on just such impressions that allowed Scholte to win from the Iowa legislature voting and office-holding rights for Pella's Dutch residents even before they had become naturalized citizens.[13] These were to be Americans who happened to come from the Netherlands, not Dutchmen who by chance found themselves in the United States.

In addition to his functions as minister, land agent, entrepreneur, and promoter of education, Scholte found time to be active in American politics. Like Michigan's A. C. Van Raalte, he supported Abraham Lincoln, whose reciprocal respect and esteem he clearly enjoyed.[14] It is indicative of Scholte's unequivocal eagerness to emerge from the cocoon of ethnocentrism and to stand and be counted among the Americans that he, unlike most publishers and editors of nineteenth-century Dutch-American journalism, chose to make his weekly *Pella Gazette* an English-language newspaper with only occasional material in Dutch. Exactly the opposite would have been the norm, but not for this enthusiastic publicist, who liked to sign his journalistic essays with by-lines such as "An Adopted Citizen."[15]

Even in his Dutch-language publications, Scholte warned against the self-righteousness of esteeming one nationality higher than another.[16] While Scholte never denied (or even encouraged denying) Pella's Dutch heritage, he did everything possible to enhance acculturation to the New World in which he had found his new homeland. He took obvious pride in the fact that English predominated in secular and sabbath schools, and envisioned the day when, in the wake of acquired linguistic facility and intermarriage with Americans, there would be "but little difference between Pella and other more exclusive American Towns."[17]

Scholte's exuberant cosmopolitanism failed to ring the death knell for the Dutch language in Pella. By 1856, the First Reformed Church of Pella had been established, thereby affording the town's Dutch-American residents a religious affiliation (in contrast to Scholte's separatist utopianism) that fostered, rather than challenged, an ethnocentric bias. By about this time, on-site reports confirm that both English and Dutch were used in the local schools; it was only in the last decades of the nineteenth century that this pattern finally and definitively shifted in favor of English.[18] There was, in other words, no bolting attempt to dismantle the cross-generational continuity of language maintenance and transmission. Rather, it appears that the community exemplified the pragmatic sort of bilingualism recommended by R. T. Kuiper in his often-cited attempt at formulating a statement on language policy for America's ethnic Dutch communities:

> Leer 't Engelsch zoo goed as het Hollandsch te spreken,
> En 't Hollandsch als 't Engelsch, zelfs zonder gebreken;
> Leer beide talen goed gronding verstaan.

(Learn to speak English as well as Dutch, and Dutch as well as English, without any faults, learn to know both languages thoroughly.)[19]

Nevertheless, the realization that the dominant culture was (and would remain) American, rather than Dutch, opened the way for that sense of self-deprecation or even outright shame that is so familiar in the history of America's ethnic communities.[20] In 1854, John F. Le Cocq of Pella published a poem in *De Sheboygan Nieuwsbode* admonishing his fellow Dutch-Americans not to be ashamed of their lineage.[21] The poem concludes with the lines:

> Dus Nederlanders, schaamt u niet
> Uit zulk een volk gesproten . . .
> En wilt door geen verkeerden geest
> Uw Vaderland verachten;
> Maar wilt haar lof en eere steeds,
> Met alle kracht betrachten.

(Hence, Dutchmen, don't be ashamed that you've sprung from such a people . . . nor with a perverse spirit despise your fatherland; but rather ever, and with all your might, accord it praise and honor.)

The poem is indicative of several points worth noting. Quite clearly some must have been inclined, even at this early date, to rush into the embrace of all things American, even if it meant laying the axe to the roots of heritage. It is also evident that there were already those who wished to contravene any such tendency, and to reaffirm Dutch language and culture in any way possible. The lines were already being drawn for a debate that simmers in some circles to the present day.

The World Comes Knocking at the Door

O NE can sift a great deal from the journalism of the earlier years of this century concerning the picture that the local Dutch must have had of Pella and of the American world beyond.[22] Much of the rest of this chapter will draw upon the record of local publications to complement and corroborate interview data.

Tied inextricably to the question of Pella's ethnic identity is that of its size and relationship to the outside. In 1901, at approximately the beginning of the period on which this study concentrates, a debate was being waged over whether the Wabash Line should be allowed to come to Pella. It was noted in *Pella's Weekblad* that "Pella will always remain what it is: a slowly blossoming but prosperous rural town . . . where the farmers come at certain times to do their shopping . . . but it will never become a large city of commerce and activity and factories (and we'd rather not have it that way, either)."[23]

Today Pella points with pride to its major industries, especially to the headquarters of the Vermeer Corporation and Pella Rolscreen. It took some years for that attitude to prevail. One source, just now entering retirement, cited several specific instances of bitter criticism that he and quite a few others recall being directed at the Rolscreen Corporation (founded in 1925) for "bringing in Americans" (i.e., to work in the factory), and the resentment felt not so very many years ago toward Central College for recruiting students from non-Dutch, nonlocal, and non-Calvinist backgrounds. Needless to say, economic prosperity from a healthy industrial base and the college's success in academic and extracurricular areas have long since led to a moderation of such sentiments.

Like many a pose of hauteur, Pella's condescending

disdain of the outside world stemmed not from genuine convictions of superiority, but rather from barely masked fears that eyes that had seen more of the world might in fact find the little town's ethnicity laughable, if not downright ridiculous. After all, even some of Pella's own found that a little bit of Holland went a long way!

A surprising number of sources openly admit that many a Saturday afternoon in the earlier decades of this century was spent teasing the *Groentjes* 'greenhorns' from the fatherland who appeared in town in outlandish costumes that belied the wearer's recent arrival. The most embarrassing stereotypes seemed to be confirmed by women in high shoes and long skirts of a conservative color and cut, and by men in wooden shoes *(klompen)* and baggy trousers. Definitely more intriguing, but no less bizarre, were the erstwhile (and would-be) sailors who sported gold earrings, a memory of which lingers in the name "Earring District" for the neighborhood on Pella's west end, where these saltier types tended to live in earlier times.[24] If Pella's natives found such manifestations of Dutch culture a bit hard to explain away, what might the outsider think, or even say? In this context, it is much easier to understand the reduced enthusiasm of some older residents for the more sentimental attempts within the community at recapturing the "Dutchness" of former times.

"Surely Thou Art Also One of Them; for Thy Speech Betrayeth Thee"— *Matthew 26:73*

A sense of reticence concerning cultural heritage naturally included a reluctance to expose that one mark of national and social background least easily explained away: natural fluency in another language (or, even worse, vestiges of the foreign language in one's command of English). Lucas correctly points out the dilemma that plagued Pella and so many Dutch and other ethnic communities. By around 1900, the paradoxical attitude had developed that, while it was considered simply "too Dutch" to try to express one's thoughts in correct standard Dutch, it nevertheless constituted an injustice to the Dutch language to propagate the hybrid, local idiom, laced with solecisms, which was used by all but the freshest arrivals from the Netherlands. The net result was that there was not a great deal of encouragement for anyone to use Dutch of any sort whatsoever as the language of choice.[25]

About this time a series of editorial essays appeared in *Pella's Weekblad* from the pen of one Solano, who dedicated a number of his columns to the question of American versus Dutch cultural loyalties.[26] In late 1900 and early 1901, Solano took on an unmistakably defensive posture toward those who had "reproached him for being too Dutch," and for forgetting that he was, after all, an American now.[27] In desperation he noted that the end result of the continuously escalating sense of shame about the Dutch heritage was that the youth of Pella had come to the point of affirming American cultural values even more enthusiastically than "the Americans" themselves.[28] In other quarters, a curiously ambivalent attitude prevailed toward the Dutch language, and some, while gently scolding Pella's residents for their rare mixture of the two languages, did so with the humor of a long-standing friend whose chiding belies familiarity or even firsthand experience, rather than scalding reproach. When Rev. Jan Keizer, a minister at the First Christian Reformed Church of Pella from 1898 to 1902, prepared a report on use of the Dutch language for Pella's chapter of the *Algemeen Nederlandsch Verbond*, his extensive and often humorous list of Anglicisms in the local Dutch was loaded with terms only too familiar to Keizer himself, who prudently declined to cast the first stone of condemnation.[29]

Any number of incidents might be cited from the anecdotal accounts of interviewees to illustrate a sense of urgency felt among the young of their own generation to acculturate linguistically; one, however, stands out as a particularly telling example of attitudes toward ethnicity and language. Between 1910 and 1915, Alice (a fictitious name for a very real person) was confronted by the primary teacher at her rural school, who informed her (in what evidently was a rather unvarnished manner) that she really oughtn't speak Dutch any more. Peers concurred fully with the teacher's imperative. Although Alice had formerly spoken Dutch with her family and schoolmates, the shock of the experience was so great that she simply ceased speaking the language, and it was soon noted, to the surprise of all, that Alice could no longer communicate in Dutch even when it would have been in her own interest to do so. Passive comprehension of the language seemed to be strangely impaired. From all outward indicators, Alice had become, through a kind of "linguistic shell shock," suddenly and thoroughly monolingual. No less striking than the incident itself is the evident reliability of those sources who have reported its occurrence.

Children were not the only ones in line for a few disparaging comments about language; husband and wife could be split over the issue. A couple who had migrated from the Netherlands some years earlier was present at one of the first celebrations of Tulip Time in the mid1930s. The husband recognized the songs, began to sing along in Dutch, and was heard wondering whether his wife might not care to join in. To this invitation he received the curt and mortified reply: "Ja, you shut up." Stung, the husband cast back the rejoinder: "Ja, *you* shut up!" Along a somewhat less humorous vein than this (possibly apocryphal) tale is the verifiable account from roughly the same period of a rural Peoria man who married a woman from nearby New Sharon. Though both came from Dutch-American families, the wife's clan had succumbed to the "Americanizing" influence of her hometown. The wife suffered such a shock when she first heard her husband speak Dutch in a perfectly natural and spontaneous manner with a neighbor that she felt compelled for some time to express doubts about the prospects for satisfactory partnership with a person given to such linguistic performances!

All this is not to say that English was acquired with ease by those who preferred not to know any Dutch. Even several highly articulate speakers recall times when their "brogue" or unconscious use of non-English modes of expression betrayed them as scions of Dutch families. One individual, who spent much of her life in professional circles, and who is an outspoken proponent of language study, lamented the fact that her own English vocabulary always suffered from a certain leanness, due (in her opinion) to too much Dutch (and too little English) having been spoken in the home by her parents.

While not always extreme, the situation nevertheless represented a classic case of schizoglossia, with speakers insecure not only in a second language, but also in the full range of possibilities for the first.[30] For many, the dilemma was compounded by the fact that the first language (from a chronological viewpoint) was frequently not the language of choice, and seldom the language of formal training.

From about the turn of the century until cessation of publication of the *Weekblad* as Pella's last Dutch-language newspaper in 1942, one finds that products naturally associated with the outside world are consistently advertised in English. These ranged from notices of rates for *Scientific American* through advertisements for Sears Roebuck and Company through testimonials to the efficacy of patent medicines. Hence, when the clothier John Dykstra took out a full-page English ad in 1899 under the heading "Read This Over Carefully: We Will Save You Money" he may well have been trying to affect the air of the sophisticated merchant at home in a more urbane milieu.[31] However one wishes to interpret the ad, it is not aimed at the unsophisticated, recently arrived and monolingual *Groentje* with his trunk full of Old World fashions. Much the same, no doubt, may be said about the headline ad placed a few months later for the "Grand Band Concert, Christmas Dinner and Supper at the Bon Ton Restaurant" featuring "Music from 11:00 a.m. till 2:00 p.m. and from 5:30 p.m. till 7:00 p.m. Oysters Served all Day."[32] For the benefit of those who wished to read English without exposing themselves to worldly allurements, the *Weekblad* Store concurrently advertised an important price reduction on "een aantal GOEDE [*sic*] Engelsche boeken" (a number of GOOD [their capitalization] English books).[33]

One of the several retired ministers interviewed in the course of my research pinpointed the earlier significance of language use quite well. There undoubtedly was a period when fluency in Dutch was more a mark of piety or a guarantee of status than it is today; even at that time, however, its use (and by implication, a speaker's willingness to espouse the traditions of the Dutch-speaking community) was valued more highly as "a check against being absorbed in the morals and the custom of the time" than as an indispensable means of effective communication.[34]

There is fairly strong concurrence on just what "the morals and the custom of the time" were. An editorial from around the turn of the century describes Saturday night in Pella ("De Zaterdagavond in Pella") as an event widely known for raucous music on the town square and wanton drunkenness that appeared "to be more on the increase than on the decrease" ("de dronkenschap is eer tedoende dan afnemende" [i.e., eer toenemend dan afnemend]).[35]

Sad as it was to see the young given over to such dissipation, the greatest fear was that an impressionable youth might undergo complete secularization, and thereby cut himself off from the faith of his fathers. The following tale, though perchance apocryphal, illustrates this fear. It has been circulated in various versions, with a range of tantalizing embellishments.

A young lad goes out into the world, losing contact with home and family. In desperation, his grandmother girds herself up and resolutely goes forth to bring the young man to his senses. Seeing his grandmother approach, the youth panics, unable to remember where he had put his Dutch Bible. Rummaging through his drawers, he is barely able to recover it in time ("die [Bijbel] kond' ie haast niet vinden," as one raconteur put it). Grandmother refuses to be fooled and blows the dust off the book ("moest de stof [i.e., het stof] afblazen van het boek"), thereby unmasking the grandson's laxness in devotional reading. Ashamed, the young man comes to his senses (i.e., realizes he must accept traditional values), and the triumphant grandmother returns with the repentant stripling in tow.

Returning to the fold clearly meant embracing certain beliefs, and possibly even certain restrictions on matters as personal as the selection of a marriage partner. Again, I would like to cite but one of several possible illustrations of this point from interview data. A source from a highly visible Dutch family in Pella who is now at the threshhold of retirement recounted his experience. He had courted American girls, but saw the marriage of a cousin to a non-Dutch girl boycotted and concluded (stating to the interviewer in an entirely nonfacetious manner) that he was not sure that marriage outside the ethnic circle "would have found much more favor than somebody getting married to a dark person." He had seen weddings in which his relatives were not invited because they were adherents of the wrong branch of the Reformed faith, and consequently decided not to cross denominational barriers in choosing his own mate. He described the then prevailing attitude among relatives from the two "camps," the Reformed Church in America and the Christian Reformed Church, as one of each side expecting the other "to stay on its own turf" ("dat [i.e., the fact that a relative espoused the other branch of the Reformed faith] is all right, maar jij blijft op je [eigen] plek!"). Not surprisingly, the informant married a Dutch-American girl with the proper denominational credentials. All indications point to equal or even greater constraints on other young Dutch-Americans growing up in the earliest years of this century.

Naturally one of the more serious arenas of flirtation with the English-speaking world was the school, and in particular the halls of higher education. Considerable attention was given by the local papers to the identification of colleges into whose care the young might safely be entrusted.

Central College seems not to have always enjoyed the local esteem accorded it so readily today. In 1902, for instance, the record had to be set straight in an article entitled "Ons [Our] Pella College."[36] It was not true (alluding to the College's earlier affiliation) that only Baptist ministers were turned out at Central. Residents of the town should quit sending money to Hope and Calvin Colleges and demand greater recognition of the good job being done at the local school. Near the end of the article, in a thinly veiled attempt to tell Central College what it could do to improve town-gown relations, the author noted that a number of ruffled feathers could be smoothed down if only the school would see to it "that a little more attention were paid to the Dutch language" ("dat ook een beetje meer op de Hollandsche taal werd gelet").

It seems to have taken Central a few years to sense the importance of the Dutch connection, but learn it did, and in time the school, which for years had been placing ads in English in the *Weekblad* (and thereby had probably been sending the signal to some that its education was another intrusive product from the American world without), ran major advertisements in Dutch. By 1916, the school reported proudly in closely timed articles that Central College, formerly of Baptist affiliation, now stood officially and firmly in the fold of the Reformed Church, and that among the more significant credentials of an incoming faculty member charged with instruction in vocal music and violin was a proficiency in Dutch.[37] These notices appeared just as pupils completing high school would be finalizing plans for further study.

More was at stake here than language maintenance. Doyle has shown that from 1850 to 1925 there was a steady increase in English and a steady decline in Dutch literacy in the Pella area, where it was the Americans, rather than the Dutch, who tended to be more highly educated and more likely to hold white-collar positions.[38] While the Dutch made steady gains as farmers and (to an extent) as skilled tradesmen, they consistently outnumbered the Americans, albeit at decreasing rates, in unskilled occupations. If a young person in Pella nurtured aspirations of a professional career, it would be necessary to seek higher education, preferably in an "approved" environment; for Central College to receive the necessary

cachet of approval (and also tuition payments from satisfied parents) it would need to demonstrate understanding
for the concerns of the ethnic community in which it was
located. One point of concern lay no doubt in the fear that
young persons might become so thoroughly Americanized
that they would reject the ethnic community that had fostered them. The most salient token Central College could
offer as an assurance of sympathy with these concerns was
support of the language whose use was still perceived by
many as the hallmark of fidelity to local ethnic traditions.
There was very possibly less concern with maintaining the
Dutch language per se than with assuring preservation of
the cultural values associated with it.

Zenith and Nadir

ALTHOUGH there is more than sufficient evidence to
suggest that it was clear by 1900 that Pella could
not and would not remain forever pristine in its Dutch
orientation, the first two decades of the century nevertheless stand out as a period of unusual ethnic solidarity
among Americans of Dutch extraction.[39] Both the beginning and end of this period are the result of major international conflicts, the Boer War and World War I.

Many of Pella's oldest residents recall the rapt attention with which their parents followed the events in South
Africa. Some even tell of plans by family members to
emigrate to Africa to support their fellow Dutchmen in the
diaspora, as it were. Though very few ever left Pella, it is
clear from articles in the *Weekblad* that the situation in
South Africa was seen as a challenge to the Dutchmen of
the world to unite in common support of a just cause.

By the end of the nineteenth century, the typical issue of the *Weekblad* featured as front-page fare a summary of international news, headed by events of note in the Netherlands and followed by reports on South Africa. Serial novels (often built around plots having little to do with current events in the Netherlands, the United States, or South Africa) appeared with such moving and patriotic titles as *Adolf en Clara, of Hoe Nederland een Republiek Werd (Adolf and Clara, or How the Netherlands Became a Republic).* By 1900, new subscribers to the paper received a promotional gift consisting of an atlas of South Africa with ten maps, six pages of text, and pictures of President Kruger, a Zulu chieftan, traditional Boer entertainment, an old Dutch residence, a gold-miner's hut, a Swazi maiden, and much, much more. In various issues of that year, one could find reports on what was said by and about Cecil Rhodes, Paul Kruger, United States President McKinley, Lord Baden-Powell, and other prominent international figures concerned in one way or another with South Africa. It didn't take long for incendiary captions to appear such as "Boer of Brit? Wat zijt Gij?" (Boer or Englishman? What are you?).[40] It is surprising that not more was made of the fact that the language encroaching upon Dutch in Pella was also the language of the foe in South Africa.

One insight gained from reading the newspapers of the period is that support of the Boer effort did not necessarily imply insensitivity or indifference to the needs of Africa's native populations. In the tradition of H. P. Scholte, who authored the earliest antislavery tract to appear west of the Mississippi River, the publishers of the *Weekblad* printed, alongside an installment of the novel *De Helden van Zuid Afrika (The Heros of South Africa),* the pleading poem "Des Negers Klacht" ("The Negro's Lament"), a call for just treatment of nonwhites.[41] (Frequent and positive comments on the potential of Africa's black peoples leads one to believe that Pella's Dutch of around 1900 would be scandalized by, and ashamed of, Pretoria's current policy of apartheid.)

A point often obscured (and certainly lost on the non-Dutch of the period) was the patently pro-American political involvement of Pella's citizens. These Dutch-Americans might have opposed certain Americanizing influences, but they were in no sense less than loyal to the government of the United States. The *Weekblad* made it abundantly clear that it was the duty of all eligible Dutch-Americans to vote, and did not hesitate to print pictures and biographical data of major candidates, along with instructions in very clear Dutch as to how one ought to mark the *Democratische* ticket.[42]

World War I brought opportunity to show concrete evidence of loyalty to the American homeland. A new round of naturalization classes was announced, with sections offered in both languages, so that any who may have been in the country for some time without having acquired citizenship could do so in the most convenient manner possible.[43] Those unable to fight could certainly buy Liberty Bonds, which the people of Pella did with zeal. In the summer and autumn of 1917, the front page of the *Weekblad* was regularly devoted to progress in the Bond Drive. (By mid-June of that year, $136,800 in bonds had been sold, and more than $1700 collected for YMCA work.[44]) Pella had every reason to share in Iowa's pride at emerging first in the Liberty Loan campaign; its citizens had amply shown (or so they thought) that they were "Amerikanen door keuze" (Americans by choice) as they were wont to proclaim at the beginning of printed advertisements for the bonds.[45] As the war progressed, the *Weekblad* published more and more biographical material on the lives of prominent American patriots, and added an American flag to the statement of ownership and publication.[46] It was, therefore, a cruel irony that the town's citizens soon came to be treated as suspect enemy sympathizers because of their beloved language.

The blow came at the hands of a man not particularly beloved in Pella, Governor William L. Harding, whose visit to Pella in 1916 as a gubernatorial candidate drew the comment from the *Weekblad* that, though a Democrat, the man spoke well but said little. "He covered up much of the truth. He presented his side [of the matter] in a slick manner, and for the man who didn't know better or didn't think for himself, he made a good presentation. His whole speech was aimed at pleasing his listeners, without saying much of importance."[47] The Pella electorate would doubtless have agreed with Derr's assessment that "Harding was bombastic. He spoke in slogans and shibboleths and avoided complexity. Among those who agreed with him, he was immensely popular."[48]

Evidently there were those who did agree with him, for in the same year he was elected Governor of Iowa, an achievement ascribed by the *Weekblad* to an inebriated electorate made up of "thousands of drunk Democrats who voted for him" ("het toont dat duizenden natte [*sic*] Democraten voor hem stemden"), or perhaps to renegades from higher principles.[49] In 1917, Harding issued a proclamation making it a crime to speak any language other than English in schools, in public places, on the telephone, in public addresses, or in worship services.[50] (Those who wished to worship in another language could do so at home, though in Harding's opinion it probably did not matter, since, as he had said, "There is no use in anyone wasting his time praying in other languages than English. God is listening only to the English tongue."[51])

Pella was cut to the quick by Governor Harding's proclamation. The *Weekblad* now summarized its past record of expressed loyalty to the United States, and even printed a copy of a statement in Dutch and English on the subject, which had been sent to President Wilson.[52] The paper complied with the requirement to publish notice of a true and accurate translation of its text on file with the postmaster.[53]

While the *Des Moines Register* led the fight to oppose the ban on foreign language newspaper publication, Lafayette (Lafe) Young, Sr., editor of the *Des Moines Capital* and an avid supporter of Harding, singled out several towns as patently disloyal, including Sully, just north of Pella in Jasper County.[54] In late 1917 and early 1918, several churches in and around Pella were visited in an attempt to check compliance with the proclamation, an event whose recollection still leaves some older informants visibly shaken. Old hostilities between the Dutch and their "American" neighbors, such as those festering in nearby Peoria, rose to the surface once more.[55]

Though Harding tried to soothe Iowa's ethnic groups by claiming that loss of ethnic language was a small sacrifice to bring in the fight to curb domestic sedition, the fact was that his unpalatable proclamation stood. Discouraged and demoralized, the ethnic groups "retreated," as Derr so aptly put it, "even from the basic American right of voting," allowed Harding to win the 1918 election, and thereby "became casualties of the war on the homefront."[56] In a word, the spirit of the Dutch-speaking community had been broken, and with the necessary revitalizing influx of new speakers from the fatherland curtailed in 1924 by federal legislation restricting the number of immigrants to this country, the necessary conditions for gradual obsolescence of the language had already been met.[57]

Some attempts were made to revitalize the language, though none enjoyed any long-term success. The most common catalyst to language maintenance cited by informants was one already firmly in place in the community: catechism class, where the Heidelberg Catechism, some passages from the Dutch Bible and Psalter, and selected points from the Canons of Dordt and the Belgic

Confession were read (and often explicated) in Dutch.[58] This class was a once-a-week affair, and at least one informant lived in an area where Dutch readings were discussed Friday afternoon in school by those children who might not be in catechism class. Even some of the children not expected to take catechism class did so for the express purpose of learning more of the language; an individual whose lifelong religious affiliation has been with Pella's small Darbyite congregation attended a Reformed Church catechism class to strengthen her Dutch.[59]

Most speakers freely admit that Dutch sermons from the period between the World Wars were a tedious business for speaker and listener alike. Some half a dozen sources offered completely spontaneous comments on the fact that, after the "English interregnum," it could finally be admitted that the Dutch of the Scriptures as preserved in the *Statenbijbel* was dated, and did not correspond to the Dutch being spoken in Pella. Many a preacher was caught in the dilemma of somehow feeling that he ought to preach in the style of the Dutch Scriptures, though this meant speaking a not altogether natural form of the language. If the preacher spoke archaic Dutch, he was sure to drive his younger hearers to English-speaking churches; if he spoke current Dutch, it might be considered an act of irreverence; if he spoke English, he had capitulated. Even the occasional *preeklezer* who read a prepared sermon text in "*Statenbijbel* Dutch" often stumbled over sentences whose tortured constuctions were known to elicit sideline comments from the sermon-reader of the sort not normally issued from the pulpit. Any way he turned, the good man of the cloth found himself in a no-win situation.

The question of language use was, however, only one part of a much larger debate over just how much accommodation to the dominant culture was permissible. Even those who admitted that loss of ethnic and national identity by the Dutch might be inevitable feared that the real loss would be one of solidarity with the Reformed tradition. Language loyalty had, in short, become a matter of affirming a particular cultural legacy whose continuation was freely (if fearfully) admitted by most to be in danger. As an editorialist noted a few years after World War I in the *Weekblad:* "Dit gevaar bestaat niet daarin dat [het volk] op den duur zijn oorspronkelijk nationaal karakter zal verliezen. Dat moet. Maar het gevaar bestaat hieren dat ons volk ook zijn Gereformeerd karakter zal verliezen. En dat mag niet." (This danger consists not of the people's loss over time of its original national character. That must [come to pass]. But the danger consists of our people's also losing its Reformed character. And that may not be.)[60]

Up to World War I, some churches had held Dutch services in the morning, with the afternoon devoted to a second sermon (which gradually moved from a once-a-month or fortnightly to a weekly service in English) and Sunday School. Between world wars, English slowly gained dominance, with the Dutch sermon relegated to the position of the less frequent order of service. By World War II, only isolated churches (such as those in Peoria and Leighton) were still felt to be strongly Dutch; the others were Dutch in heritage, but only so in language for special services. To this day, it is not uncommon for a few words to be spoken in Dutch or a Psalm to be sung in Dutch at the funeral of an older person, though this custom is less commonly observed today than it was a decade ago.

Between World Wars there were a few young persons who tried to revitalize the language, though for these speakers the language's attraction lay in the vitality of Dutch as it was spoken in the Netherlands. By a few years after World War I, Central College's Dutch Club was "meeting with good success," and reported as much active participation as any of the other clubs.[61] For a period, Dutch was spoken in various young people's societies, though with time this practice also waned. Toward the end of the 1920s, a recent graduate of a Dutch university received a pastorate in Pella, and one source reports that she went not merely to hear what this dashing young man had to say, but how he said it, in Dutch of a sort not heard before in Pella: "When I was eighteen or nineteen we had a minister in our church who had just returned from the Netherlands. He had just finished his thesis and beside that he was a brilliant student. We still had three services on Sundays. The afternoon service was in Dutch so my [relative] and I faithfully attended. I'm ashamed to say that it was more to learn some modern Dutch than it was to worship. I don't suppose it did any harm. The minister . . . was very proud of the fact that his degree was earned and not honorary."

Unfortunately, momentum was not sustained. With the advent of another war, and cessation of such regular support to language maintenance as publication of the *Weekblad*, it seemed only too natural to think of Pella Dutch as a language that had run full course.[62] While most older speakers recall a potential danger during World War II of Dutch being thought of as some kind of un-American language, and therefore hesitated to use it too overtly outside a circle of regular fellow speakers, there really was not the tension of linguistic loyalty suffered during World War I. The issue had already been effectively decided: the American language was English, the language of the Netherlands was Dutch, and the language for a particular speaker pool (so long as it might continue to exist) was Pella Dutch.

And herein lies a key to much of what has happened to Dutch in Pella. Then, as now, Pella's speakers felt that their traditional language was rich and beautiful (*rijk, schoon, aardig, zuiver*); it was, however, no longer the language of the Netherlands, and those young persons who stood in a position to spearhead a movement toward revival and rejuvenation realized this. If an attempt was made to speak Dutch with (the diminished number of) newly arrived immigrants, the native Pellan found as often as not that those who arrived between the wars (and definitely those arriving after World War II) wished to Americanize as quickly as possible, and were more eager to learn English than to perpetuate Dutch.

Speakers born during or after World War I typically feel that their Dutch is not good enough to be worth perpetuating; when faced with the prospect of speaking with a person who knows Dutch only as it is spoken in the Netherlands today, they are reticent. Many find it unnatural or even uncomfortable to converse with younger persons who have taken formal training in Dutch at a college level. One older resident confided on a tape prepared by one of my assistants that he felt uneasy about speaking for members of the academic community, even though he had spent much of his professional life in those circles, and concluded: "Ik wil Webber dit niet laten horen. . . . Wij hebben hier Amerikaans Hollands." (I don't want to let Webber hear this. . . . [and then in a somewhat apologetic tone] What we have here is American Dutch.) Fortunately, the source relented and allowed me to hear the tape.

The youngest local speaker I know who acquired Dutch naturally in a home environment is now in his mid-thirties, at least a decade (and on the whole an entire generation) younger than most other speakers of Pella Dutch. He and several others of parenting age have attempted to pass on some Dutch to their children. Without an active speaker pool in which to interact, however, these children will almost certainly be carriers of the last vestiges of what once was the community's dominant language.

PART THREE

The Language

Photo by Les Sadler

Reminders of the Dutch presence include early streetscapes in the Historical Village, several windmills, a cornerstone, and—poignantly—many gravestones inscribed in Dutch.

Photo by Philip E. Webber

Pella Dutch and Its Speakers Today

EVEN in a primarily sociolinguistic study, one must eventually address the question of just which form of a language is spoken in the community under investigation. Does Pella Dutch appear to have maintained any forms that have lost currency in the Netherlands, or to have witnessed the development of unusual or characteristic new forms? Would the language spoken in Pella be intelligible to persons from other Dutch-speaking circles in the United States and abroad? In other words, from a descriptive point of view, what are the special features of Pella Dutch and how does it compare to the language accepted in the Low Countries today as standard Dutch?[1] Before answering these questions, however, we need to address several other points to establish a context in which to approach an analysis of the language.

Who Perpetuates the Language in Its Final Stages?

PERSONS from the Netherlands on tour in Pella often comment that the Dutch spoken here is old-fashioned, and their assessment is generally correct. After all, the community has lain outside the mainstream of the world's Dutch-speaking population for close to a century and a half. Hence, some speakers will occasionally add an outdated inflectional ending to an indefinite article, give an older disyllabic value to a current monosyllable (*omme* for *om*), or simply use vocabulary that has lost its currency in everyday speech. There are, however, reasons other than isolation from the Netherlands that account for these phenomena.

In part, the antiquated forms of Pella Dutch are a natural result of the self-selection by its last active generation of speakers. Born after World War I, many come from families that recognized the inevitable dominance of English and, in some cases, actually discouraged the use of Dutch. All, however, were thrown by choice or by chance into contact with an older speaker for whom Dutch was the language of choice (or indeed of necessity), and, much more important, virtually all are essentially outgoing, gregarious individuals who enjoy and habitually seek out contact with persons of different generational or social strata. It can hardly be overemphasized how strongly the marked personality type of these last speakers of Pella Dutch recalls the "inordinately inquisitive" individual, reported in studies on terminal speakers and semispeakers of other obsolescent language communities, "whose most important factors in [the] acquisition of the [non–dominant-culture's] language" are "insistent curiosity and . . . demand for linguistic inclusion."[2]

The various accounts of language transmission to a final generation of speakers are familiar enough in kind to even a casual observer of second-language acquisition: a certain child remains home longer, thereby enjoying prolonged contact with Dutch-speaking parents or grandparents; death in the family occasions a monolingual grandparent's sharing the residence of children and grandchildren; a speaker raised in homes where Dutch served only as the parents' secret language rises to the challenge of "cracking the code" and relishes the thrill of using the language as a means of identifying with the family members who wield power on the home front. Whatever the circumstance, it was typically the child with the greatest inclination toward socializing with the older generation, rather than the child with demonstrated scholastic aptitude or marked native endowment, who tended most readily to learn Dutch.[3]

Fully as often as not, an individual from outside the immediate family circle (e.g., the hired hand) offered the young speaker a crucial role model. The glowing reports of ways in which these linguistic mentors initiated the upcoming generation into the lore and mysteries of the adult world indicate that fluency in Dutch was only one part of an entire constellation of personal traits emulated by the fledgling speaker.

The events most readily recalled by current speakers as occasions on which Pella's rugged individualists of preceding generations persisted in using Dutch are characterized by a conspicuous absence of participation by any pantywaists or sissies. As one speaker (whose parents rarely spoke Dutch with him) tells it: "both [a neighbor and his brother] were in our threshing [crew], and they'd quite often be speaking Dutch, and so did [the operator of the threshing rig], . . . I think mostly it was the fact that they were of an age [at which they could enjoy conversing together], and they had an opportunity to talk Dutch, where they probably didn't talk it at home, but when they were together they did. They'd talk a lot of Dutch, the threshing ring. At coffeetimes, at dinner, you know, we'd have big dinners. Whenever they were sitting in the shade waiting for something." This individual went on to make it clear that whoever wanted to hold his own with "the big boys" of the threshing crew simply had to speak Dutch.

A somewhat more humorous example of how Dutch

was felt to belong to the adult world comes from a speaker who reminisces: "I guess I recall going to Oskaloosa with Dad in the old Model A years ago, and then he would meet some of his brothers or brother-in-laws [sic] and so forth—you know—and they would stand there on the street and talk Dutch—you know—and then they would have a little off-color story once in a while, thinking, well, that little guy [the informant] doesn't know what they're talking about, but I knew everything they said." Decades later, many a "little off-color story" is remembered in strikingly vivid detail.

It would seem from various accounts that this final generation of speakers, unlike earlier ones, never really experienced a full-blown period of "linguistic adolescence" in which young speakers consciously tested the language norms of the older generation, developed new forms of its own, and adopted the innovations of the peer group. Rather, the linguistic behavior that often enjoyed greatest acclaim by the peer group was precisely the ability to speak like an adult. Since the role models and conversation partners for these developing speakers were seldom recent arrivals from the Netherlands, the net result was that Pella's youngest speakers (a few of whom are, in fact, already retired) learned their Dutch from persons whose contact with the Dutch of the Netherlands had been via individuals now either elderly or already deceased. It is therefore not at all surprising that Pella Dutch impresses visitors from the Low Countries as quaintly anachronistic.

The Tone of a Typical Conversation

OLD-FASHIONED does not, however, mean prudish. Humor is a major part of any extended conversation in Dutch, and the investigator who speaks the language is soon treated to tidbits not easily had in this ostensibly conservative community where virtually no business establishments are open on Sunday and certain individuals admit a preference for buying their alcoholic beverages and doing their dancing in outlying communities.

Some of the humor is harmless enough and could as easily be conveyed in English (though not with the same flavor, informants hasten to add). A retired minister tells of three young chaps who see an elderly gentleman coming down the street and decide to make fun of his age. The first greets the old man with "Goeie avond, vader Abraham" (Good evening, father Abraham), the second with "Goeie avond, vader Isaak" and the third with "Goeie avond, vader Jacob." The old man replies that he is not Abraham, Isaak, or Jacob, but rather "Saul, de zoon van Kis" (Saul, the son of Kish) who has come "om de ezels te zoeken" (i.e., in search of his father's asses, cf. 1 Sam. 9); the old man concludes triumphantly "en ik heb d'r al drie gevonden" (and I've already found three of them) and goes on his way.

Other stories, though easily understood in English, nevertheless come out of a particular cultural context. Smoking, for example, has become so much a part of Dutch life that there is even a proverb " 't is geen man, die niet roken kan" (he is not a man who cannot smoke), and one traditional gift by a bride to her groom is a fine pipe. Nevertheless, not all wives get a great deal of vicarious pleasure out of their spouses' smoking, including one who acidly wondered of her husband, in the presence of house guests, "Moet je dat verrekte ding al dadelijk aansteken?" (Must you light up that blasted thing so quickly again?), to which the husband coolly replied, "Ja, mijn lieve vrouw; gerookte vlees verderft [i.e., bederft] niet zo gauw" (Yes, my dear wife, smoked meat does not spoil as quickly).

Some other humor might leave a casual observer with the impression of a certain propensity for the prurient within the Dutch soul; after a decade of speaking with Pella's Dutchmen, however, I have concluded that they are simply so glad to find someone with whom they can converse in Dutch that they readily show their delight (and confidence) by saying things said otherwise only in trusted circles. To interpret the jokes and anecdotes otherwise would be to misconstrue the sense of closeness the speaker often attempts to establish with the investigator.

Much of the more playful humor is innocent bathroom banter, often presupposing familiarity with both languages, and frequently derisive of persons with incomplete fluency in one language or the other. An immigrant writes home in an attempt to persuade his brother to come to America, assuring him that he will offer his services in helping the brother to make a good beginning in the new land, noting "Je bent in America all right, maar je moet een goede *start* hebben" (You'll be all right in America, but you need to have a good start). Today *start* has made its way into the Dutch language as a loanword; it is not a part of the Pella Dutch lexicon, however, and speakers who retell this incident expect the hearer to associate *start* with Dutch *staart* 'tail, tail end'. Numerous other examples might be cited of bilingual wordplay that presupposes a familiarity with the Dutch terms for body parts and bodily functions.

Even when seemingly impervious to other stimuli, Pella's Dutchmen can respond to a touch of earthy humor.

A hospital aide working in the geriatric ward attended a minicourse in Dutch that I offered several years ago. She had picked up *achter* 'behind' and *kant* 'side', and fairly bubbled with enthusiasm as she told how a cranky patient unwilling to receive an injection in the hip laughed and rolled over when she jocularly asked him (in such Dutch as she had at her command) to show her his *achterkant*. On a small scale, the aide was demonstrating exactly the kind of jocund and easy social interaction, often across generational lines, that characterizes Pella's final generation of speakers.

In addition to humor, the conversation is frequently spiced with proverbial observations and folk wisdom. On occasions when I interviewed several persons simultaneously (e.g., a husband and a wife who found it more convenient to schedule a single interview), one speaker would often drop a bit of lore and the other would respond with a well-known saying, only to be met by some proverbial offering of the first speaker, and so forth, for several "rounds." Both the spontaneity of recall, and also the large stock of popular lore at the command of the average speaker, make it clear that such material constitutes an important part of the linguistic heritage of the informants.

One hears several distinct categories of proverbs and folk wisdom, and none is more common than sayings having to do in some way with the weather. (As one individual put it: "I'm always thinking about weather in Dutch some way or other.") Much of my interviewing was completed during the early spring of 1983, when any number of interviewees reminded me that "maart [die] roert zijn staart, april doet wat hij wil" (March moves (i.e., swishes) its tail, and April does what it wishes) or that "aprilletje zoet geeft soms een witte hoed" (sweet little April sometimes gives us a white hat). (See Figure 3.1.) When I caught a ride home during an April rain shower and the

Fig. 3.1. Cartoon illustrating some of the problems of trying to maintain cross-generational continuity of language use.
(Reprinted by permission, from Ed Le Cocq.)

sun was making every effort to break through the clouds, both the driver of the car and one of the passengers broke out simultaneously with "als de zon schijnt op de wegen, komt morgen weer regen" (when the sun shines on the [wet] streets, there will be more rain again tomorrow). Barely mentioning rain in passing on another occasion prompted the observation: "regen [in current Dutch usually: kring] om de maan, zal het wel gaan; regen [viz. kring] om de zon, water in de ton" (rain (i.e., mist) around the moon, and the weather will be nice; rain around the sun, and there will be water in the barrel).

The naturalness with which such lore is recalled and disseminated is shown by the ease of many speakers in improvising on or augmenting a popular saying (such as the one about "sweet little April" cited previously). As I prepared to leave one interview, a disgruntled speaker observed that still another April snow shower was on its way: "Ja aprilletje zoet, die draagt nog wel dikwijls een witte hoed" (Yes, sweet little April sure enough often wears a white hat—which, incidentally, the investigator also noted as he returned home that afternoon with snowflakes on his cap). Such popular lore consists, in other words, not merely of commonplaces that have been mindlessly repeated any number of times, but rather, in many instances, of expressions intentionally chosen and often reformulated to convey a speaker's thoughts and feelings at a given moment.

I've asked several sources whether they recall any weather lore that, in retrospect, seems to have been mere superstition. Most cannot, and the response of one informant typifies the attitude of those few who do. The hired hand working on the speaker's childhood farm seems to have been "very particular" about the "verkeerde tijd van de maan" (the wrong phase of the moon); as the interviewee thought about the character of the hired man, however, he concluded that there probably never really was very much credence placed in the importance of lunar cycles, and that a great deal may have been made of the matter simply for the sake of "passing it along" to eager and curious youngsters.

Almost equally popular are moral admonitions, such as the frequently heard "waar je mee om(me) gaat, daar ben [or: word] je mee besmet" (you bear the mark of whatever you associate with). Here, too, one encounters freely improvised variant forms, such as "waar je mee naar bed gaat, daar ben je mee besmet" (you'll bear the mark of whatever you go to bed with). The list could go on almost indefinitely, to include such time-proven wisdom as "gauw en goed zijn twee dingen" (quick and good are two different things), "vroeg begonnen, veel gewonnen" (early begun, much won), "eens mans dood is des and'ren zijn brood" ["de een z'n brood is de ander zijn dood"] (one man's death is another's bread), etc. One modest informant, a retired schoolteacher, demured about offering me any proverbs before she had a chance to give the matter some thought. Shortly after the initial interview she called to tell me that she'd jotted down "a few bits of good advice," and then recited a list that ended up filling three pages of notes in my files. Obviously, there is no dearth of typically Dutch folk wisdom in circulation among speakers of Pella Dutch.

Less frequently encountered, but definitely evidence of deep-seated fluency in the language, are riddles and puzzles, such as:

> De boeren in het Noordenland
> Hebben tien vingers op elk hand
> Vijfentwintig op handen en voeten
> Zeg nou hoe wij dat lezen moeten.

On a literal level, we are told that the farmers in the north have ten fingers on each hand, five and twenty on their hands and feet. How can this be? The last line challenges us to read the poem (i.e., divide the lines) in such a way that they make sense. (The farmers in the north have ten fingers / on each hand five / and twenty on their hands and feet.)

On one occasion I was told of an object out in the pasture consisting of two poles, on which sat a barrel, on which sat a pivot, on which sat a ball, on which there was a forest (or: sheaf, shock?) with all sorts of creatures running around in it. What might that be? ("Achter in de pasture staan twee palen, op die palen is een ton, op die ton is een draaiom [sic], op die draaiom is een bal, op die bal is een bos, en in die bos [presumably, in terms of the informant's own explanation of the riddle: dat bos] lopen alle kleine kriepertjes [kruipertjes]. Wat is dat?") The answer, of course, is a person with lice in the hair.

One also encounters idioms whose literal meanings reflect a bit of unpretentious, folksy wisdom about the ways of the world. In one interview a speaker came to an abrupt stop in a narrative about other persons, winked at me and said "Ja, dat muisje heeft een staartje" (yes, that little mouse has a tail, [i.e., there is more to that story; more is yet to come out of what we've been discussing; this will have consequences]). On another occasion, a good-natured customer on my son's paper route complained that the new prices for a month's delivery asked for "de huid met de staart" (the hide along with the tail, [i.e., all that one can give]).

Finally, there are children's rhymes on such timeless themes as reciting the ABCs: "A B C / De kat gaat mee / De hond blijft thuis / Piep zei de muis / In het zomerhuis [usually: voorhuis]" (A B C / The cat goes along / The dog stays home / The mouse said "peep" / In the summerhouse [entrance-hall]), the wages of tattling, "Klikspaan, Klikspaan [or: boterspaan] / Durft niet op straatje gaan [alternately: door mijn straatje gaan] / Hondje zal je bijten

/ Katje zal je krabben / Haantje zal je pikken / Dat krijg je voor je klikken" (Tattletale, Tattletale [Butterscoop] / You don't dare go out on the street [through my street] / The doggie will bite you / The kitty will scratch you / The little rooster will peck at you / That's what you get for your tattling), and going to bed, (recited as one holds up the various fingers), "Naar bed naar bed zei Duimelot / Eerst nog wat eten zei Likkepot / Waar zal ik het halen zei lange Jaap / Uit vaders kastje zei Korteknaap / Dan zal ik [alles] zeggen zei Pingelasje / Dat jij gesnoept hebt uit vaders kastje" (Off to bed said Thumbkin / First let's eat something said Lick-a-pot / Where shall I get it said the Long Chap / Out of Dad's cupboard said the Short Fellow / Then I'll tell all said Pinky / That you snacked out of Dad's cupboard). Though less frequently recited, phrases and lines from such rhymes do occur from time to time in the speech of sources who recall them from a period when they were much more common than they are today.[4]

Whatever Else It Is, It's Dutch![5]

IN broad outline, the phonological patterns of Pella Dutch are those of standard Dutch (or, in some literature, ABN: *algemeen beschaafd Nederlands*). Even the variants that one finds are recognized as regionally or socially acceptable alternatives to "standard" forms. Hence, for example, it is not unusual to encounter the typically Dutch loss of intervocalic [d] after a long vowel or diphthong, as in *da[d]elijk* 'right away', *verschei[d]en* 'various', *gehou[d]en* 'held (past participle)', etc. Almost equally common is the introduction of an epenthetic [d] between continuants ([l], [n], [r]) and a vocalic [r], as in

Herwijnder for *Herwijner* 'person from Herwijnen', or *benden* for *bennen* '(variant form) are'. (More will be said later in this chapter about regional variations and vestiges of dialect forms.)

The verb exhibits very little variation from standard forms, except in the fairly pervasive regularization of the verb *zijn* 'to be', which appears with at least some frequency in the speech of most informants as *ben / bent / bennen* (or, for speakers with more eastern accents, as *bin / bint / binnen*). In addition, the infinitive of the same verb appears rather more commonly than in the Netherlands in the antiquated form *wezen*, as in "[a certain individual] was niet fit om een dominee te wezen" (i.e., was not fit to be a preacher).[6] In isolated instances a hypercorrectional plural ending appears on athematic verbs, (e.g., *we gane(n)* for *we gaan* 'we go'); even more rarely an intransitive verb compounded with a separable prefix omits -*ge*- in the past participle: "de kerken die van Holland afkomen [*sic*] waren" (the churches of a Dutch background). In a single, isolated instance I recorded *gong* as the preterite of *gaan* 'to go'.[7] Finally, while most speakers make a correct choice between *hebben* 'to have' and *zijn* 'to be' as the auxiliary for forming the compound past of verbs, one occasionally encounters an incorrect choice, especially with the verb *zijn* 'to be' itself (e.g., *had geweest* for *bin geweest*). In at least some instances, the context of the sentence suggests that the speaker may have formulated the incorrect verbal phrase on analogy with an English past perfect 'had been'.

The most notable feature of the noun is that it is frequently an English loanword, as discussed in greater detail in the final section. Two items in plural formation do, however, merit note here. On the one hand, local speakers follow the pattern of standard Dutch in maintaining the singular form of nouns such as *jaar* 'year' and *dollar* 'dollar' when the plural merely indicates approximate extent, rather than exact and full measurement (e.g., "vijf jaar geleden," [five years ago] rather than "vijf jaren," where five *full* years are indicated). On the other hand, they deviate from the norm in occasionally failing altogether to use a plural ending where it is needed (e.g., "vijf kind" for "vijf kinderen" [five children]).

Like their linguistic cousins in the Low Countries, Pella's speakers of Dutch are less than consistent in the use of inflectional endings on adjectives. (Only a few approached consistency, and even fewer correctness, on this point.) The situation is more or less typified by the speech of one informant who, within a few sentences, used the phrase *een groot man* without adjectival inflection both in the correct sense (a great man) and also in the sense that would demand adjectival inflection (a large man). As a synonym for *veel* 'much, a lot' one frequently encounters colloquial *een hoop* (literally 'a pile'), as in "een hoop schik" (a lot of fun). Among the neologisms used as adjectives, the one occurring with some frequency was *afscheidisch*, 'schismatic, (and hence) contentious' from *afscheiding*, '(religious) separation, schism', a term much used in connection with the religious separatist movement with which the town's founder, H. P. Scholte, was associated.

Along with the regularization of the verb *zijn* 'to be', the most striking nonstandard (though not therefore unfamiliar) feature of the language is the pervasive use of the slang pronoun *hullie*, 'they (all)'. Formed on analogy with familiar second person plural *jullie, hullie* is well known in the Netherlands as a form that an educated person would not readily use in public; in Pella, even discriminating speakers use the pronoun freely. One speaker from a background in the eastern provinces made isolated use of the possessive pronoun *hum* 'his': "op hum schoot zitten" (to sit on his lap).

Several other aspects of pronoun usage merit note. *Ietwat* 'something' seems to enjoy a fairly active life, bordering at times on direct competition with more universally common *iets*. In addition, the particle *er* occurs almost as frequently in the form *d'r* as in the somewhat more usual form *er*. This is true both in those instances where *er* goes back to an older genitive plural form ("ik heb d'r al drie gevonden," [I've already found three of them]), and where *er* is derived from *daar* ("ik ben d'r verantwoordelijk voor," [I'm responsible for that]).[8]

The one notable feature of adverbs is the truly Dutch propensity for the use of diminutive forms on nouns that have become part of fixed nominal phrases used in pronominal or adverbial function. The most common example, where the underlying noun is no longer felt to have any function except as part of a fixed modifier phrase, is *een beetje* 'a little bit'. In Pella, and in particular among certain speakers, this process continues to be a highly productive one for the formation of adverbial elements. For example, "je moet eens een keer*tje* komen" (you'll have to come one 'little' time), or "hij lag daar . . . voor een poos*je*" (referring to a veterinarian who had been kicked unconscious by an animal: he lay there . . . for a 'little' while). All of these forms are possible in Dutch, and their noteworthiness lies not in their unusualness, but rather in their frequency of use in the local community.

Sooner or later, an investigator is bound to notice the highly varied range of tone represented by the interjections of Pella Dutch. On one hand, the variegated terms of abuse (*je oude lamzak, jij mieter, potdorie, smeerlap, paardedief* and its variant based on the name of a local proprietorship *paardeko(o)per*, etc.) could singe the ears of even the most hardened. On the other hand, one occasionally hears among fairly conservative speakers *ja ik* for affirmative "yes I do" and *ik nee* or *nee ik* for "no I don't'—forms that, it has been suggested, perpetuate the language of the formulaic and pious answers to the queries of the Heidelberg Catechism.

In sum, the range of variations exhibited by Pella Dutch is one possible within the scope of what is coventionally accepted as belonging to the Dutch language. Pella Dutch is not on the verge of becoming a true separate language (such as Afrikaans), but rather is exactly what its name implies: the Dutch language in the form commonly encountered in Pella, Iowa.

Vestiges of Dialect[9]

SOONER or later, in almost any discussion of the language itself, one hears the word *tongval* 'dialect' (literally, the way the tongue falls in the mouth). There is an almost formulaic structure to the course that the conversation takes. First of all, it is reported that in earlier days one heard regional distinctions much more clearly than today, and also one simply heard more said about difference of dialect ("Daar hoor je niet zo veel van . . . vroeger wel!" [You don't hear so much about it now . . . though in earlier times you certainly did!]).[10] One is then assured that the person being interviewed is no expert on dialects, but would nevertheless be willing to offer a few examples of helpful shibboleths by means of which one can tell the origin of a speaker's dialect. (A comparison of these dialect benchmarks with the situation actually encountered in the interview process constitutes the material for most of the remainder of this section.) Finally, speakers may share an example or two of regionalisms in their own speech, or that of their family. Usually these examples are quite specific, as in the account of a local woman who first traveled as a mature adult to her ancestral homeland in Gelderland, in the region between Zutphen and Steenderen. Initially, the natives of the village were a little skeptical as to whether the Americans were really in the right part of the Netherlands, since none of the local folks recalled any families with the names in question having emigrated to the United States. Language and speech patterns soon changed that. "We were walking along and we heard a wren [Dutch *winterkoninkje*] and my sister said 'och daar is een toenekriepertjie' [viz. *tuinkruipertje*] and this woman laughed and said 'now I know that you folks are from Gelderland because only we would say that, and not only that, but only in a small region [of Gelderland] would they say that'."[11]

Some dialects are only sparsely represented among those speakers who qualify as sources for this study (i.e., a given dialect may be spoken locally, but primarily by recent immigrants). Hence, we are told by local speakers mimicking the once more commonly heard dialect of Zeeland that "de Zeeuwse *tale* / is de beste *tale* / van allem*a*len" (i.e., Zeeland's is the best of all languages) with long open medial [a] strongly fronted and palatalized, approaching the vowel of English *Sally*, just as one would expect for this dialect. Except for the imitators, however, I could not find a "pure Pella" informant for the Zeeland dialect[12]. Much the same must be said for the dialect of Drenthe, represented by a single speaker whose case is a special one on several counts: those characteristics of his speech that reflect an origin in Drenthe were acquired outside Pella, and the source (who guardedly offered what may in fact have been samplings of his own personally idiosyncratic speech as "samplings of his dialect") has systematically attempted to minimize all regionalisms in his speech to boot.

If any dialects appear to have lost footing in the local

speech community, they are those of Groningen (represented in great part by speakers from rural backgrounds) and Overijssel (with an epicenter of migration around Nijverdal). Speakers of these dialects are, within the current speaker pool, invariably offspring of "mixed marriages" in which parents spoke the Dutch of different regions; in the process of establishing a dominant home speech pattern, neither the dialect of Groningen nor that of Overijssel seems very often to have come out on top. Among Groningers, the diphthongization of *boek* 'book' to *bouk* and of *steen* 'stone' to *stain*, as well as the monophthongs of *wies* for *wijs* 'wise' and of *hoes* for *huis* 'house' can be detected, though with greatly varying intensity and consistency. Speakers from families in Overijssel tend simply to produce generally eastern forms, though not always (or even primarily) forms specifically associated with the speech of that province. The retention of earlier [l] in *old/ald* for *oud* 'old', which one might expect to encounter in the speech of persons from this far east in the Netherlands, is absent altogether.

While not particularly numerous, speakers of the dialect of Utrecht have nevertheless managed to hold their own, perhaps precisely because theirs is a central dialect, sharing characteristics of the dialects both of Holland to the west and of the provinces to the east.[13] In Pella, the Utrechts dialect forms a link between the Dutch of the relatively few speakers from South Holland, whose speech is conceded to be "good, pure, beautiful" (and yet somehow almost artificially antiseptical) Dutch ("het goede, zuivere, mooie Hollands"), and the easily identified, well-represented and yet often decried and deprecated speech of Gelderland. The characteristics of Utrechts that predominate and maintain their currency in Pella include: standard Dutch [a] appearing as a low back rounded vowel in *dacht* 'thought (preterite)' and *opgebracht* 'brought up, reared' (with the locally understood meaning probably

influenced by English *brought up*, but see note 5); standard Dutch [e:] in *veel* 'much', *spelen* 'to play', *zeven*
'seven' as *veul, speulen, zeuven; ben* 'am', *denk* 'think' as
bin, dink; the [o:] of *door* 'through', *voor* 'for' as *deur,
veur;* diminutives with a long final vowel (e.g., *kindjie* for
kindje 'little child'); occasional confusion of *liggen* 'lie' and
leggen 'lay'.[14]

Simply because of the sheer number of speakers in
Pella, the dialect most often imitated, and also most
severely maligned, is that of Gelderland, and in particular
of the village Herwijnen. One cherubic-looking Pella resident known for his wry humor looked me straight in the
eye and assured me with no trace of a smile that he had
become so accustomed to the so-called Hell-wijnders (viz.
Herwijn[d]ers) and their dialect that he had only recently
realized that it was the Herwijns dialect, rather than the
rest of the Dutch language, that was different!

There doesn't seem to be a great deal of distinction
made in the minds of many Pella residents between general Gelders and Herwijns, and from a descriptive point of
view it is often difficult to draw a sharp line of distinction
between the two.

Like the speakers of Utrechts, especially Eastern
Utrechts, Pella's speakers of Gelders (often Gelderland Ve-
luws) will also pronounce *door* as *deur* and *zeven* as
zeuven. Even more than the speakers of Utrechts, they
prefer diminutives with *-jie* or *-ie: kindjie* 'little child',
kopdoekie 'little head covering'. In addition, they frequently pronounce *De Bruin* as *De Broen* and *krijgen* 'to
get' as *kriegen* (i.e., with long monophthongs rather than
dipthongs). The second-person singular familiar pronoun,
especially in interrogative sentences with forms of the verb
zijn 'to be' is *gij/ge*: "zijde ge gek?" (are you crazy?).[15] The
vowel of *water* 'water' may appear as a low, rounded back
vowel, as will the vowel of the modal verb *moet* 'must'.
Quite frequently, *dartien* replaces *dertien* 'thirteen', and

Har(re)wijns takes the place of *Herwijns* 'dialect of Herwijnen; having to do with Herwijnen'. Especially among speakers from near Herwijnen, *paard* 'horse' is pronounced as *peerd*, and *geen* (negation of the indefinite article), *beetje* 'a bit' as *gien*, *bietj(i)e*. (It is unclear whether the small but consistent group of these speakers who regularly say *viertien* and *viertig* rather than *veertien* 'fourteen' and *veertig* 'forty' do so as part of a regionally conditioned speech pattern, or because they have succumbed to the pressures of analogy and have regularlized the forms on the basis of the simple cardinal number *vier.*) In the idiolect of a single speaker with a father from near Limburg's German border, *negen* 'nine' and *wegen* 'ways' were regularly pronounced as *neigen* and *weigen*. Both *hebt* and (to a lesser extent) *heeft*, forms of the verb 'to have', appear as *het* or even *hee*.[16] Finally, there is a great deal of lexical preference (e.g., *kop* for *hoofd* 'head' and *meui(e)* for *tante* 'aunt'.

English Has the Final Word[17]

A S shown by the bastardized language of newspaper ads, Pella's Dutch-Americans have been relying upon English vocabulary and English modes of expression (albeit with a superficial veneer of Dutch lexicon) for at least as long as any currently living speaker would be able to remember.[18] Purists of the Dutch language must have died a thousand deaths to read of "Men's en Jongens Strooien Hoeden" (Men's and Boys' Straw Hats) advertised in absolutely ungrammatical Dutch, which ignored the fact that the language admits a suffix as a signal of possession only after proper nouns, and in a phrase of this sort demands the use of a preposition (these are straw hats *for* men and boys).[19] Only a person fluent in English could possibly begin to guess what the noun *goederen* 'goods, property, possessions' is supposed to mean in an advertisement for "Bed spreien" (bed spreads) and "Dress Goederen en Trimmings" (dress goods and trimmings).[20]

The process continues to the present day, and examples are almost endless of ways in which the penetration of English into a speaker's Dutch has caused confusions great and small, often with humorous results.[21] Almost every speaker of Pella Dutch who has traveled to the Netherlands has a favorite anecdote to match or top the account of one prominent individual who absolutely wanted the privacy of her own bathroom while touring abroad. Familiar with neither the convention nor the vocabulary of a WC separate from the room in which one bathes, she politely but firmly requested a room "met eigen bad" (with its own bath). To her chagrin and amusement, she received a room with private shower, while still having to share the lot of all the other guests, using a common toilet facility at the end of the floor on which her room was located.

Pella's linguistic melange is no doubt the result of habit, and usually amenable to correction if a speaker is simply reminded to choose a Dutch word. During one interview, for example, a gentleman remarked that a certain neighborhood boy "brengt hier de paper" (brings the paper here); his wife offhandedly mentioned the Dutch noun *de krant* 'newspaper', and hardly skipping a beat, the husband picked up the thread of his narrative "brengt hier de krant 's morgens" (brings the newspaper here in the mornings) and went on to the next topic.

There are, nevertheless, certain English nouns that persist even in the speech of speakers who are otherwise fairly consistent in the correct choice of Dutch forms and vocabulary. Apart from words that are simply the products of cultural differences between Pella of the twentieth century and the Netherlands of the late nineteenth century, one notes a recurrent corpus of English terms for which a perfectly good Dutch equivalent is available. Nouns firmly entrenched in Pella Dutch include *shape* (both as 'physical form', and in the expression "in goeie shape" [in good shape]), *farm(er)*, *cousin* (*neef* and *nicht* are known almost exclusively in the sense of 'nephew' and 'niece'), *store*, *dishes* ("it's always been dishes for us"), *community*, *country* (both in the sense of 'nation' and also 'rural land'), *part*, *dress* (possibly to avoid the multiple meanings of *kleed*, which in some contexts can refer to clothing in general), and *experience* (both in the sense of an individual event through which one has lived, and also the sum total of what one has learned in a particular area of activity). Almost equally well represented are interjections such as *you know*, *sure*, *all right*, and many, many more. Most speakers use *plenty*, and a striking number rely on *same* to do the work of *(de) zelfde*.

There are any number of verbs borrowed from English, but relatively few that cannot be explained in terms of simple cultural-chronological considerations. There is, however, no particular reason why so many speakers lack a verb 'to travel' (*op reis gaan*) or 'to hurry' (*opschieten* or *zich haasten*, not *hurryen* as is sometimes heard here). In autobiographical accounts by informants, Dutch *verhuizen* 'to move (from one residence to another)' is rare; most speakers prefer to use English *move* with any Dutch morphological endings that might be needed. A fair number of adverbs have been taken over from English, including many of the compounds of *some-* (e.g., *somewhere*) and *any-* (*anyway*, etc.). Surprisingly, not all speakers prefer extremely common Dutch *boven* and *beneden* for 'upstairs' and 'downstairs'. Some borrowed adverbs may simply represent less frequently expressed concepts, as suggested by sentences such as "de anderen trokken automatically toe" (the others came along automatically).

As illustrated by the example of *hurryen*, the easiest thing to do when a verb is needed is to add a Dutch ending onto an English lexical unit, thus yielding *fixen, clearen* and *claimen* (land), *shoppen* ("de vrouwen lijken te shoppen" [women like to shop]), etc. Frequently an adverbial particle in English becomes a separable verb prefix in Dutch (e.g., *opfixen* 'to fix *up*', and *uitfig(u)ren* 'to figure *out*, to find a solution').

Sometimes it is the English mode of expressing a concept, rather than English vocabulary per se, that is borrowed. Almost everyone in Pella graduates from the *hoge school* 'high school', even though the term in standard Dutch implies a university-level educational institution. One seldom hears Dutch *gewoonte* 'custom' and virtually never *manier* 'manner', though one often hears *weg* 'way, street' used as though it had the semantic range of English *way* as a rendering of these two words: "als het de Hollandse weg is" (as is the Dutch way/custom of doing things); " 't Is een machtig mooie weg om te travelen" (it's a mighty nice way/manner in which to travel).

When a local merchant wasn't sure what the word for spark plug was, he suggested *vuurstok* 'fire rod'; his brother, who was also present, proposed *aansteker* 'igniter'. Both were plausible attempts (none, including myself, realized that standard Dutch uses a loanword, *bougie*). One person present in the store showed his reliance upon the process of literal translation by coining the term *vuurstopper* 'fire stopper'. It took me a moment to realize that 'stopper' was here meant in the sense of a plug in a car's engine.

Any number of English words have been taken over phonologically intact into Pella Dutch. Among the frequently used English loanwords, however, there are certain sound patterns that yield more readily than others to the influences of Dutch pronunciation. The process depends not only on the sounds of the borrowed word, but also, at times, on its orthographic representation in English.

A central vowel with the grapheme *u*, for instance the vowel of *truck*, will often be rounded and raised slightly, as in Dutch *truk*; if, however, the vowel precedes [l] plus another consonant, it is usually pronounced [o]. (When I brought in a failing flashlight to the local hardware, the clerk lost no time in identifying the problem: "jongen, de bolb is kapot" [boy, the bulb is no good].) The pronunciation [o] is also the usual one for English words with the vowel [a] represented by the grapheme *o*): the past participle *gestopt* 'stopped' is pronounced exactly as it is in the Netherlands (despite the fact that speakers of Pella Dutch, who tend to think of *gestopt* as an example of the nonpurity of their own speech, are shocked to hear that speakers in the fatherland have also adopted this Anglicism into the "real" [*sic*] Dutch language).

What we have come to call "long *u*" in English, as in Huber (the name of a street in Pella), will frequently be pronounced with the vowel of Dutch *sturen*, (i.e., with no on-glide and as a strongly fronted high-rounded vowel). The vowel of English *catch* as a loanword in Pella Dutch is almost always pronounced with the Dutch vowel felt to be the closest approximation to that of the English word (i.e., with the lax short vowel of Dutch *pet*); this is true even if the speaker has no tendency to use that same vowel (as do some speakers of regional American English) in pronouncing English *catch*. Finally, English [g] is usually given the fricative pronunciation represented by the Dutch grapheme *g*. Hence, English *grade* (in school), with a backing and lowering of its vowel, is pronounced exactly like Dutch *graad* 'degree', paving the way for semantic confusion of the sort to be discussed.

If Dutch morphological endings appear on a borrowed word, any phonological rules that might apply in standard Dutch are also operative in Pella Dutch. Hence, if *dress* is given the diminutive ending *-je*, the final [s] is palatalized, just as is the final segment of *zus* '(familiar) sister' when it acquires the diminutive marker and appears as *zusje*.

Verbal lexemes in Dutch that end in a voiceless segment must use a voiceless suffix (if a suffix is called for) in the formation of the past participle. Since English follows the same principle, it is not too surprising to see it in force in *gestopt*, cited previously. What is more noteworthy is the fact that Dutch, in contrast to English, requires no suffix if the lexeme ends in an alveolar stop [d] or [t], and indeed speakers of Pella Dutch avoid the use of any spurious suffix in these cases: "toen ben ik op de railroad gestart" (then I started on the railroad).[22] Since, in such cases, English requires not only a suffix, but in fact an added syllable to mark the presence of the suffix (start*ed*), it is easy to tell which language's rules the speaker is following.

If a speaker from the Netherlands feels that Pella residents no longer truly speak Dutch, it is probably because of the presence of so many loan homonyms, that is, Dutch words that have acquired the (often quite different) meaning of the English word with the same (or at least a fairly close) pronunciation. To recall an example given earlier, *graad* 'degree (of temperature, of geometric measurement, etc.)' is regularly used as a rendering of English 'grade (in school)', even though this is not at all the Dutch convention (the appropiate word would be *klas* 'class').

Thus one hears *lijken* (intransitive) 'to seem' used to translate its near-homonym in English, (transitive) 'to like'. Some speakers simply fail to respond at all to standard Dutch *houden van* 'to like, to be fond of'. One even hears *lijk* (standard Dutch 'corpse') as though it were English preposition-or-conjunction *like*: "praat ik niet lijk een Gelderlander?" (don't I speak like a Gelderlander?). Dutch *drijven* 'to impel' has taken over for *rijden* as the verb 'to drive (a car)': "hij drijft de car en hij is nat" (he drives the car and he is wet/drunk).[23]

Other verbs influenced by similar-sounding English forms included *menen* and *groeien*. Dutch *menen* might be translated 'to mean' in expressions such as "meen je wat je zegt?" (do you mean what you're saying?) or "hij meent het goed" (he means it well). In Pella it is also used like English to mean in the sense 'to signify', (e.g., "ik weet niet wat dat meent," [I don't know what that means] for Dutch "ik weet niet wat dat betekent"). The verb *menen* also occurs locally rather more frequently than Dutch *bedoelen* in the sense of 'to intend', as in "wat meen je?" to express "what do you mean to say?" (i.e., "wat bedoel je?"). In English, 'to grow' may be either transitive or intransitive, but in Dutch only intransitive. In local parlance, however, one hears Dutch *groeien* used as a transitive verb (e.g., to express the concept of growing vegetables).

The examples of borrowed words and borrowed meanings could go on almost indefinitely: *schot* is used for 'shot' in the specific sense of 'injection'; *paal* 'stake, post' is used for poles of all sorts (fishing poles, fence poles, etc.); the interjection *nou* 'now' is used rather more frequently than Dutch *nu*, possibly under the influence of near-homonymic English *now* ("nou en dan eens" [once in a while now and then]). It is even possible that some of the confusion between *liggen* 'to lie (repose)' and *leggen* 'to lay' in Pella Dutch may have English roots. One speaker from outside the (admittedly rather expansive) territory in the Netherlands where one would normally expect to find confusion of the two, produced sentences such as "hij legt te slapen" (literally: he lays sleeping). True, the semantic crossover of the two forms is widespread among speakers of Dutch. It is at least reasonable, however, to suspect interference from a weak distinction in American English between the concepts of 'to lie' and 'to lay' as a contributing factor to this hybrid pattern.

PART FOUR

Conclusion

W HILE the general process of linguistic acculturation to the dominant norm is a well-attested phenomenon in the history of America's countless ethnic enclaves, the specific details of the situation in Pella are unique and deserve to be recorded not only in lingustic literature, but also (and not least of all) in a manner that makes them accessible to members of that community who may someday wish to recapture a bit of a now-vanishing era.

There is currently a great deal of scholarly activity in the field of language contact and language change. As the final pages of this book are being written, several major collections of essays are being prepared for press, with reports on case studies that, in greater and less detail, will strike a chord of familiarity with the reader of this volume. James Dow of Iowa State University, for instance, has compiled a rich array of studies for a special two-volume number of the *International Journal of the Sociology of Language* on language maintenance and language shift. Nancy C. Dorian of Bryn Mawr College is editing a volume for Cambridge University Press, entitled *Investigating Obsolescence: Studies in Language Contraction and Death,* with sections on both the cultural and linguistic aspects of language change.

If there are any points that set this book apart from others, it is that it is the first book-length study based on prolonged on-site contact of the interaction between the Dutch and English languages in this country and one of a relatively small number of longer works that combine the fruits of language investigation with observations on patterns of community life within a prominent ethnic center of the American heartland. (For an excellent overview of Dutch throughout the United States, see Jo Daan's recent *Ik was te bissie . . .*; for the Great Plains states in general, one might profitably consult Paul Schach's collection of shorter papers, *Languages in Conflict.*)

It would tax reader and author alike to pour through a list of all the sociolinguistic studies of recent years that in some way suggest the very broad scholarly context in which *Pella Dutch* is presented. In addition to various collected studies, one can choose individual sociolinguistic treatments of languages as diverse as American creoles, Serbian in Louisiana, or the idiom of America's Judeo-Spanish community.[1] Those with a particular interest in Dutch will find a rich variety of data on the current linguistic situation in the Low Countries.[2] While much of the current literature includes some technical and descriptive material, many authors nevertheless attempt to place their findings into a social and cultural context that can be appreciated by seriously interested nonspecialists.

It would be a pity, however, if this study were to end with an encouragement to look elsewhere for a final statement on just what the material presented here really means. Consistent with my desire that this be the account given by my sources themselves, I would like to conclude with a remark that, though made quite casually by a member of the speaker pool, says ever so much about the current and future status of the Dutch language in Pella. In the Netherlands, one might have said "er is wel nog meer, maar ik weet niet hoe men het alles in het Nederlands zou moeten zeggen." In his Pella Dutch, this individual said "zo binnen wel meer dingen dat ik nie weet hoe moet men het in het Hollands zeggen" (there are certainly more things [to tell], but I don't know how one ought to say it in Dutch). Having made that admission, the speaker concluded not only an interview, but also gave expression to the end of the era in which Dutch was the natural language in which to express whatever was worth telling.

Appendix A

QUESTIONNAIRE

(All information, especially that of a personal nature, is
voluntary.)

Your name:_____
Your place of birth:_____
Your place(s) of residence:_____
_____
Your sex:_____   Your age (approximate)_____
Address:_____Phone:_____
_____
Your occupation(s):_____
_____
Have you had any special schooling or training?_____
   If so, what kind:

Do you speak any foreign languages?_____Which one(s):

How many generations back did your family come from the
Netherlands?

How many grandparents were from the Netherlands?
When did they come to the United States?
How many grandparents were of Dutch extraction?   Which side?
Did they speak Dutch?

How many parents were from the Netherlands?
When did they come to the United States?
Were any of your parents of Dutch extraction?   Which side?
Did they speak Dutch?

Have any of your relatives gone back to the Netherlands?
Which one(s)?

How frequently do they go, or when and how long were they there?

Particulars (as tourist, to visit relatives, work, study, etc.):

How many relatives have come back to Pella to live after being
away for a number of years? relatives:_____   myself:_____
Any particular details? (how long were you or they gone, for
what reasons, etc.)

Are you aware of the province(s), city or cities, town(s) where
your relatives in the Netherlands come from?_____specifically:

Where do you now have relatives or personal contacts in the
Netherlands?

With whom do you still keep contact?

Do you personally think of yourself as ethnically Dutch?
    strongly_____   moderately_____   remotely_____

Was Dutch spoken in your home when you were growing up?_____
When?
By whom?
Did you also speak it?
Who taught Dutch to you?
Who spoke it with you?
Who encouraged you to speak or learn it?

Did you teach Dutch to your children, or has someone else? Who?

Did you ever learn Dutch in school?_____When?
What school?
Did you ever have a teacher that taught in Dutch?
Any particular subject(s)?
Did you ever have Dutch textbooks?
Did you also speak it in school?

Did you attend a church which held services in Dutch?_____When?
Where?   RCA or CRC? (optional)_____

How often was the service in Dutch or English? (or was only the
sermon in Dutch?)

Did you speak Dutch while at church?

Did you ever use Dutch at your place of employment?
Did you use it with coworkers?
With employer?
With customers?
With sales people?

Was Dutch ever spoken in certain societies, clubs or
organizations?
When?
Particulars: (church groups, ladies aid, consistory, Tulip Time
committee, etc.)

Do you recall any specific occasions other than those mentioned
above when Dutch was generally spoken, e.g. festive occasions
like weddings and parties, or special family activities and
celebrations?

Check the box that is appropriate for you.
Do you presently use Dutch when speaking:

	always	usually	often	some-times	never	does not apply
1. with parents						
2. with grandparents						
3. with spouse daily						
4. with spouse when angry						
5. with spouse when children are present						
6. with children						
7. with children when angry						
8. with in-laws						
9. with older siblings						
10. with younger siblings						
11. with close relatives						
12. with classmates on playground						
13. with classmates in school						
14. with best friends in public						
15. with best friends in private						
16. with minister						
17. at work with boss						
18. at work with employees						
19. with acquaintances						
20. while shopping with sales people						
21. at religious services and meetings						
22. with girl/boyfriend in public						
23. with girl/boyfriend in private						
24. with doctor						
25. with teacher						
26. with neighbors						
27. with households pets						

Have you ever subscribed to a Dutch newspaper?
If so, which one(s):

Do you correspond with anyone in Dutch? Whom?

Do you converse in Dutch with anyone not mentioned above? Whom?

	never	some-times	often	usually	always	does not apply
1. I read Dutch books.						
2. I read Dutch in the newspapers or church bulletins.						
3. I read the Bible or Psalms in Dutch.						
4. I listen to Dutch sermons or church service broadcasts.						
5. I use Dutch in my correspondence.						
6. I use Dutch with my fellow workers.						
7. I pray in Dutch.						
8. I dream in Dutch.						
9. I curse in Dutch.						
10. I count in Dutch.						
11. I make telephone calls in Dutch.						
12. I speak to people from other areas of the U.S. in Dutch.						
13. I discuss local affairs in Dutch.						
14. I discuss national affairs in Dutch.						
15. I discuss religion in Dutch.						
16. I discuss finances in Dutch.						
17. I discuss health in Dutch.						

All things being equal, would you prefer Dutch or English:

Dutch   English

_____	_____	for proverbs, sayings, etc.
_____	_____	to make plans for a trip.
_____	_____	when recalling your most memorable events of childhood.
_____	_____	when talking to a personal confidant about how you feel.
_____	_____	when talking about the news in the paper.
_____	_____	to tell a joke.
_____	_____	to make a derogatory comment.
_____	_____	to greet a friend on the street.
_____	_____	to say something intimate.
_____	_____	to say something private in a crowd.

What do you perceive to be the main advantages of speaking Dutch: (for yourself, or if you don't consider yourself a fluent speaker, for those who are fluent).

advantage in family life?_____specify:_____
_____

advantage in Church?_____specify:_____
_____

advantage in social life?_____specify:_____
_____

advantage in community?_____specify:_____
_____

advantage in business or work situations?_____specify:_____
_____

advantage in other areas:_____
_____
_____

Do you think there are any disadvantages of speaking Dutch in the above or other situations?

    Area: Disadvantages:

_____   _____
_____   _____
_____   _____
_____   _____

APPENDIX A

Check the correct column for the reasons which seem important or unimportant to you to learn Dutch:

	very important	important	unimportant	no opinion
1. It's broadening to have more than one language.				
2. To be able to enjoy Dutch music better.				
3. Dutch is a very rich and expressive language.				
4. No one can understand Pella properly without Dutch.				
5. To feel more a part of the community.				
6. To be able to read books in Dutch, e.g., the Bible.				
7. It's useful to have a "secret language" that not everyone else understands.				
8. Some of my friends and neighbors speak Dutch.				
9. To be able to understand programs broadcast in Dutch.				
10. To be able to talk to Dutch speakers from other parts of the U.S. in Dutch.				
11. To participate in Dutch dance or music groups.				
12. Dutch is a beautiful language to hear and speak.				

Should Dutch be preserved in Pella?_____Why or why not?

How or where should Dutch be preserved?

	yes or no	how or in what situations?
family	_____	_____
schools	_____	_____
church	_____	_____
community	_____	_____
organizations	_____	_____
other	_____	_____

In situations where Dutch is or was spoken, how effective and/or important do you feel it was in:

keeping family together?_____
for instance:

instilling religious or moral values?_____
for instance:

transmitting awareness of Dutch heritage?_____
for instance:

Can you give specific examples of:

    "Yankee Dutch":

    individual words "only possible in Dutch" that express your moods, feelings, etc.

    Dutch sentence constructions or grammatical types in English

    phrases, proverbs, etc.

    names of physical objects which were common household terms

    children's lore

PELLA DUTCH

Can you recall any situations which were so serious, that you felt you simply had to handle them in Dutch or in English, even though you would have had the choice of either language?

Do you feel that someone who has a strong pride in his/her Dutch heritage is more likely to be fluent in the language?

Is the person who is fluent in the language more likely to have a strong sense of pride in his/her Dutch?

Would you be biased toward a candidate for public office who spoke Dutch?

Would you prefer to buy from someone who advertised in the newspaper in Dutch, or who now is willing to conduct business in Dutch?
Comments:

Do you feel that there is any particular status in the community or other social advantage enjoyed by the fluent Dutch speaker?
Comments:

As you've responded to this questionnaire, have you had any other thoughts or recollections which you feel might help us, which you would like to share?
Thanks very much!

Appendix B

IN 1982, the author was one of the contracted fieldworkers hired to document selected efforts at ethnic heritage and language education efforts for the American Folklife Center of the Library of Congress. The report that follows represents the sitation found in Pella in 1982; specific facts may not be current, but the vast majority of the issues raised here are.

A REPORT ON ETHNIC HERITAGE AND LANGUAGE EDUCATION IN PELLA, IOWA

prepared for the American Folklife Center of the Library of Congress

by

Philip E. Webber
Central College
Pella, Iowa

1982

IDENTIFICATION OF PRINCIPAL INFORMANTS

(Code numbers in parentheses refer to archival holdings, such as taped interviews and photographic material, in the American Folklife Center's archives.)

The Historical Perspective

Mrs. Emma Lou Heusinkveld: retired teacher; author of a history of the Pella Community (ES82-PW-C8a, b)

Miss Dena Versteeg: retired teacher who formerly offered a program in Dutch to her pupils (ES82-PW-C10a)

The Pella Community Schools

Mr. Merlyn Vander Leest: principal, Lincoln School; author of a monographic thesis on the influence of Pella's Dutch background on educational programs (ES82-PW-C13a)

Mrs. Ruth Brummel: music teacher at Webster and Lincoln Schools (ES82-PW-C1a)

Mrs. Muriel Kooi: teaches fourth grade at Webster School; heritage program based on her book, *The Path of Delft* (ES82-PW-C2a, b, ES82-PW-C5b)

Mrs. Jeanine Van Vark: teaches third grade at Webster School; organized a program on Pella's history, with songs in English and Dutch, for senior citizens at Fair Haven (ES82-PW-C5a)

The Christian Schools

Mr. Ivan Groothuis: principal, Pella Christian Grade School (ES82-PW-C4a)

Mr. Fred Kooi: music teacher at Pella Christian Grade School (ES82-PW-C3a, b)

Mrs. Harriet Zylstra: librarian and resource coordinator at Pella Christian Grade School; teaches Dutch when offered (ES82-PW-C9a, b)

Mr. Al Bandstra: teaches fifth grade at Pella Christian Grade School; does a unit on local history (informal interview)

Miss Anne Gritters: student at Pella Christian High School; former Dutch pupil of Mrs. Zylstra (ES82-PW-C11a)

Private Efforts

Mr. Robert De Jager: retired teacher-principal of the Peoria, Iowa, Christian School; now offers private instruction in

Dutch (ES82-PW-C6a, b, ES82-PW-C7a, b, ES82-PW-C14a, b)

Miss Lori Schiebout: pupil of Mr. De Jager (ES82-PW-C11b); Mrs. Marie Schiebout: Lori's mother, present at the time of Lori's inteview (EW82-PW-C11b)

Mrs. Katherine Schiebout: Lori's grandmother; arranged for her granddaughter's instruction in Dutch (EW82-PW-C13b)

Mr. Len Gosselink: parent of Holly Gosselink, one of Mr. De Jager's pupils and a pupil at Pella Christian Grade School; proprietor of a Christian book store (ES82-PW-C12a, b)

Dutch Family Singers and Dancers: a cooperative of families interested in practicing and performing Dutch music; prominent at Tulip Time and at festivities throughout the year (ES82-PW-C4b)

Persons and Programs to Watch

Mrs. Millie Vande Kieft: responsible for summer programs at the library; this year initiated a program in Dutch children's literature and Dutch proverbs and sayings (ES82-PW-C15)

Mrs. Barbara Dieleman: emeritus professor of education at Central College; long-standing association with the schools; chair of a college-community committee to celebrate 200 years of formal ties between the U.S. and the Netherlands (informal interview)

Miss Gail Franje: student at Pella Christian High School who took private lessons in Dutch from Mrs. Zylstra and went to the Netherlands on her own initiative

Focus and Scope of the Report

The Pella, Iowa project centered not upon a single school per se, but rather upon the varied attempts of a community with a strong ethnic heritage to transmit cultural values and practices to its younger members. Case studies and assessments are based upon observation of programs taking place both within and outside formal educational settings. In considering the activities of the community's public and parochial schools, we have focused upon programs which clearly go beyond the mandated curricula.

Evolution of Community Attitudes toward being Dutch-American

Pella was founded in 1847 by a group of religious separatists from the Netherlands, under the leadership of the charismatic Rev. H. P. Scholte. In addition to being a minister, Scholte gained prominence as an entrepreneur, publisher, educator and politician. Had his foreign birth not disqualified him for the position, Scholte would have been Lincoln's choice for an ambassadorial post in Austria. The well-nigh palatial home of Rev. Scholte still stands in impressive grandeur on the north side of the town square; its interior and contents have enjoyed painstaking curatorial care under Mrs. Martha Lautenbach, justly regarded as the community's most knowledgeable member in matters of local history. A reconstruction of Scholte's church, with original baptismal font and pulpit, stands on the edge of Pella's Historical Village, where homes and stores of the early period house artifacts and memorabilia of the community's founders, and provide the setting for various cultural activities discussed below. Several of Scholte's descendants have achieved a prominence of their own in the town's civic, educational and social circles.

Pella received its name from the Near Eastern town which provided early Christians with a haven of security from persecution, and is often referred to, both formally and informally, as "The City of Refuge" (most recently in the title of a documentary film about the town's considerable Asian immigrant population). While it may have been a city of refuge for Scholte and his followers, Pella was by no means a center of encapsulated isolation from the world of the new homeland. Throughout much of its history, Pella has shown remarkably little of the sentimental longing for the fatherland which pervades so many ethnic communities, and from the beginning, its leaders have fostered the acculturation of the town's residents to the new setting in which they found themselves. One familiar story (whose historical veracity has been questioned, but which, even if apocryphal, indicates just what is considered plausible for the period and person in question) tells of an attempt by Scholte to gain permission for his followers to recite the Pledge of Allegiance in Dutch, so that no time would be lost in acquiring American citizenship. A prolific writer, Scholte signed many publications produced in his new homeland with such by-lines as "An Adopted Citizen."

The idea that Holland had definitely been left on the other side of the ocean was enforced by events early in this century. While Iowa was relatively slow to enact legislation banning the use of foreign languages during World War I, it more than compensated for its late start by approving what is generally regarded as one of the most severe laws in the country. Virtually any use of a language other than English, in contexts which could be considered public, constituted a crime. Older members of the community recount with visible emotion the experience of being in church on Sunday when an inspector appeared, unannounced, to check on compliance with the law. In a word, it was dangerous to be Dutch.

It was also embarrassing to be Dutch! Waves of immigrants arrived around the time of World War I, and these *groentjes* (greenhorns) are remembered primarily for their persistence in wearing outlandish costumes (e.g., baggy pants), overwhelmingly rural orientation (whereas Pella was firmly established as a commercial center), and (real or imagined) opportunism, perceived as detrimental to the town's characteristic spirit of communal interdependence. Still other problems arrived with influxes of immigrants during the Depression, and after World War II. In each instance, a relatively homogeneous community's assured understanding of proper Dutch values and attitudes was challenged by the values and attitudes of real, live Dutchmen from the fatherland, and in each instance the local Dutch-*Americans* exhibited a certain defensiveness, and a subsequent disinclination to embrace the fatherland's culture with anything approaching unbounded enthusiasm.

Impact of Community Attitudes on Ethnic Heritage Programs

The pervasiveness of such attitudes toward the culture of the Low Countries only began to abate with consistency in the generation of persons now in their early forties. As a result, those who undertook programs in ethnic heritage education had, at least until recently, to face the dilemma of needing to choose between transmitting Dutch culture (though it may be imported, at times even intrusive, and frequently foreign to the local experience), and perpetuating Dutch-American values and practices (which often enough strike a native of the Netherlands as quaint, antiquated, or even bizarre).

This point may be illustrated by two items commonly associated with ethnic groups, dear to the heart of Pella's residents, and included in at least some of the programs studied here: food and music.

The typical childhood diet of Pella's older residents did not admit of great variety, and might consist of bread dipped in melted lard and sorghum molasses for breakfast, potatoes, meat and red cabbage for the main noon dinner, and an evening lunch of leftovers, perhaps with buttermilk porridge and molasses cake. Festivities such as Thanksgiving might provide occasion for *Jan-in-de-pan* (pancakes). Such a diet was dictated as much by local conditions as by any Dutch culinary traditions, and even the bologna which has made Pella famous in central Iowa was introduced by a German. This does not mean that typically Dutch foods are unfamiliar to Pella's residents. On the contrary, two bakeries with Dutch specialties do a healthy business, and no festival is complete without *poffertjes* or *oliebollen* (varieties of fried baked goods). As Mrs. Zylstra stated in her interview, there is a certain status accorded to housewives who can prepare authentic Dutch meals. As enthusiastically as such meals are received, however, they do not necessarily replicate the cuisine of grandmother's kitchen, and the young person who acquires the recipe for a typically Dutch dish may well provide grandmother with a few surprises.

Pella has been consistently supportive of musical activities. Rev. Scholte's wife was a conservatory-trained vocalist, and for a time the town supported an opera-house. After the Civil War, Pella was the home of the renowned Light Infantry Band. To the present day, the public and private schools offer superior musical programs, and the town abounds in musicians of all sorts, many of whom participate in an annual series of summer concerts, or play in the college-community orchestra. Dutch hymns and folk-songs are heard from the carillons located at the Tulip

Tower, and on the Central College campus. For older members of the community, however, whose main musical experience in a Dutch context was the singing of the Dutch Psalter (until rather recently, the only form of hymnody in the Christian Reformed Church), it comes as a surprise—albeit perhaps a pleasant one— to learn that the melody of our Thanksgiving song "We Gather Together" is actually that of a Dutch hymn, or that the pleasant little tunes coming from the carillon, the street-organ used during summer *kermis* (carnival), and the Dutch Family Singers and Dancers strolling the streets at Tulip Time are indeed genuine Dutch music.

More often than not, the import wins out over local tradition. The summer *kermis* and December *Sinterklaas* festivity (during which the good Saint Nicholas arrives on horseback, accompanied by appropriately clad attendants, and meets out the year's just deserts to the community's children in accordance with ancient and prescribed practice), though instituted only recently, have become permanent items on the town's calendar. These celebrations have no antecedent in local experience, and indeed—as several Dutch journalists have pointed out—are more genuinely Dutch than our Tulip Time, and may even be celebrated here with greater fidelity to older traditions than what one might experience in much of the Netherlands!

Other examples of typically Dutch features which have firmly established themselves in the community are the program of Dutch fronts (authenticated facades required of new or renovated buildings in the commercial district), and zeal for authentication of Dutch costume designs which, according to informants such as Mrs. Heusinkveld and Mrs. Zylstra, goes beyond anything witnessed in previous decades. The reasons for the popularity of such "imported" Dutch cultural features are several: at the crassest level, they appeal to popular clichés of life in the Netherlands; they are accessible to interested parties, whereas much of the local tradition is not (it is only this year that the author of this report began, under a grant from the Iowa Humanities Board and the National Endowment for the Humanities, to collect such frequently-unrecorded data as proverbs, superstitions, recreational habits and culinary practices recollected by the town's oldest citizens); finally, there appears to be an uneasy realization by the generation of persons now in their prime that the "good old days" out of which local Dutch-American tradition grew may not in all instances merit uncritical acceptance and perpetuation as such.

Hence, I can understand, but cannot entirely concur with, occasional expressions of disappointment that one does not find more typically Dutch art or craft activity in Pella (though some forms, such as panel painting and lacework, have enjoyed a phenomenal resurgence of popularity), that greater use is not made of specialty foods, or that more homes do not exhibit identifiably Dutch interiors and decorative schemes (a situation which is clearly reversing itself). For better or for worse, these are simply not the aspects of Dutch culture which Pella has chosen—at least until recently—to perpetuate.

If the main emphasis is not on the Low Countries' physical culture, there is certainly no energy spared in transmitting those values, attitudes and behaviors perceived by the community as its true Dutch heritage. On several occasions, my Ethnic Groups class has administered the Ethnic Identity Profile, a questionnaire which, in effect, asks respondents to assign relative "weight" to such factors as family background, language facility, church affiliation, community involvement, etc., as indicators of "greater or less Dutchness" in the eyes of the townsfolk. Responses to this questionnaire, as well as comments written in the margin or shared with the investigator, and current interviews with persons such as Mrs. Heusinkveld and the two principals, Mr. Groothuis and Mr. Vander Leest, make it clear that the espousal of these values give as clear a signal as the display of any physical object that one has enfranchised himself as a member of the community. One is frequently reminded (as we were on the evening of our arrival in Pella) that an "American" who embraces these values enjoys greater acceptance and mobility in the community than someone "from a Dutch family" who does not.

In great part, these values are associated with, or at least reinforced, by Pella's preponderantly Calvinistic persuasion. (About two-thirds of the town's churches, and probably a greater percentage of church-goers, are affiliated with some branch of the Reformed movement.) This fact is reflected in a ruggedly staunch Sabbatarianism which is not only accepted, but indeed willingly fostered, by a visible majority of Pella's residents. On one occasion, when I flagged in my zeal to complete all of my yardwork by Saturday evening, I was lovingly but rather firmly reminded by a neighbor that this was not just another day of the week, but *de grote voorzondag* (the great pre-Sunday), the period of preparation for Sabbath rest.

Also highly prized is an incredible attention to fiscal detail. Often mistaken for avarice, this actually reflects, as noted by Mrs. Heusinkveld and others, a compelling need to be in control of those things which have been entrusted to us, and by which we shape, at least in part, our own destinies. At the bottom line, the attitude is one of responsible (Christian) stewardship, and is reflected in a number of other behaviors common in the community, such as the housewife's seemingly excessive attention to cleanliness. (Sweeping, dusting and window-washing several times during the week, whether seemingly necessary or not, is by no means uncommon.)

Related to the concept of stewardship is a sense of communal interdependence. As pointed out by Mr. Gosselink, a member of the town's citizenry will simply not be allowed to founder, and all should be assured of unflinching aid, should disaster intervene. A visible example of responsibility accepted is the local hospital, built and expanded primarily through solicitation of local funds (which, unlike monies from the governmental sources, would not obligate the hospital board to answer to anyone except members of the local community). In the same context, it is noteworthy that several informants (Mr. Gosselink, Mr. Kooi) chose to cite teamwork as a main benefit of Tulip Time, rather than a great opportunity for "displaying one's wares" or for commercial gains. Finally, it might be noted that what is often mistaken for noseyness on the part of townsfolk may actually be an expression of concern about one's welfare, and an affirmation of the fact that help is available if needed.

For all of these values, family life is considered the appropriate and proper model, and it is no coincidence that school administrators and teachers report well-nigh incredible levels of parental support. Hence, it comes as no surprise that, in the transmission of those values which, to the residents of Pella, are indeed indicators of ones "Dutchness," the community's institutions (including its schools) have enjoyed repeated success.

An Overview of Pella's Schools

The Pella Community Schools had a total enrollment during the 1981-82 school year of some 1600 pupils; the Pella Christian Schools, which offer programs from kindergarten through high school, had a total enrollment of about 700 pupils. (Pella's total population is approximately 8000.) Although the Christian Schools resist the label "Christian Reformed Schools," the fact remains that Christian education was one of the main issues leading to the split between the Reformed Church in America and the Christian Reformed Church, that most Christian Reformed families do try to send their children to the Christian Schools, and that the majority of pupils in that system are from families associated with the Christian Reformed Church. Mrs. Kooi is probably correct in pointing out that the greater visibility which the Christian Schools seem at times to enjoy in the area of heritage education may be due as much to the homogeneity of the pupils' ethnic and religious background, as to any particular efforts on the part of teachers or administrators. Mr. Groothuis, principal of the Pella Christian Grade School, was quick to admit that his job is made considerably easier by the commonality of experiences and goals of his pupils' parents.

For this report, I have chosen to highlight one program of the Pella Community Schools system (a heritage-awareness unit), an offering of the Christian Schools (the Dutch language), and the parallel music programs of the two systems. I have also prepared an overview of opportunities for the study of language, folklore and music outside formal school settings.

The Path of Delft:
A Case Study in Historical Fiction vs. Fictitious History

Mrs. Muriel Kooi teaches fourth grade at Pella's Webster School. She is a person whose many talents and awesome energy have won respect throughout the community. An active member of the Pella Historical Society, she now sits on that group's board, and has accepted various committee assignments. Demonstrating the zeal of one who has made the community her own by choice, rather than by birth, she has actively promoted some of Pella's most successful ethnic-heritage programs, and was responsible in great measure for instigating the celebration of Pella's highly successful *Sinterklaas* festivity.

Perhaps most important of all, she has been supportive of colleagues in their efforts. One example is her outspoken support of Mrs. Jeanine Van Vark, whose reading group took important first steps toward a goal expressed by several informants (Mr. Vander Leest, Mrs. Brummel, and others): greater direct contact between pupils in the schools and the community's senior citizens. Activities such as Mrs. Van Vark's program on Pella's history, including a selection of songs in Dutch and English presented to residents of Fair Haven (a local retirement center), is seen as the sort of preliminary contact needed to facilitate greater involvement of our older citizens, perhaps even as occasional classroom resource persons.

In addition to her other activities, Mrs. Kooi is a prolific author. One successful series of articles, for *The Iowan*, featured a number of Pella's architectural landmarks. Her most widely read work, however, and the basis for her heritage-awareness unit, is *The Path of Delft*, a work of historical fiction whose title refers to a well-known incident in Pella's early history. Rev. Scholte's refined and cultured wife was—to put it mildly—taken a bit aback by the primitive conditions encountered upon arrival in (what was to become) Pella. Opening a chest containing her precious Delftware, she discovered that the dishes, like many of her expectations, had been irretrievably broken. The pieces, however, were saved and used to pave a pathway through the formal gardens of her new home. Some years ago, pieces of the pathway were discovered by workers on the highway which runs past the Scholte House. The possible metaphoric meanings of the pathway have remained vivid for Pella's citizenry.

Not far into the new calendar year, Mrs. Kooi begins a series of readings and discussions of *The Path of Delft*. Attention to things Dutch will already have been aroused by Mrs.

Kooi's own enthusiasm, and by previous units, such as the production of *Hans Brinker*. Perhaps most exciting for pupils, however, is the series of some half a dozen walking tours, during
which children are invited to reinact the experiences of the
book. The exact itinerary varies from year to year, but typically
includes: a retracing of the final leg of the immigrants' trek to
Pella; a tour of Pella's shop-windows, which display early
Dutch and American *realia* prior to Tulip Time; a visit to the
local graveyard, which includes a remarkably successful unit on
culling historical and cultural data from the gravestones; a trip
through Pella's Historical Village (to learn, as Mrs. Kooi put it,
that there is more there than just the boyhood home of Wyatt
Earp); and a tour of the Scholte House.

During her interview, Mrs. Kooi confirmed what I had already gathered from casual conversations with her pupils: the
schoolchildren are far more interested in history than fiction,
and that historical fiction (i.e., a plausible retelling of what may
well have taken place), is much preferred over fictitious history
(platitudes and clichés about the founding fathers which, with
little or no change, could serve as the presumed common historical background for members of virtually any ethnic group
founded by immigrants). This preference for historical perspectives is a fine indicator of the success of Mrs. Kooi's work.

When asked what they liked about the *Path of Delft* unit,
pupils responded with remarkable uniformity: the material is
local, tangible, theirs to share in whether they are Dutch-American or not, and not distant or foreign. This does not mean,
however, that Mrs. Kooi is more committed to promoting a
"local" understanding of Dutch culture than an "imported"
Dutch version. As stated in her interview, she staunchly favors
an infusion of Dutch culture into all programs, across the curricula. Mrs. Kooi spent the summer of 1982 in the Netherlands,
collecting material (and at that, very contemporary and distinctly Dutch, rather than Dutch-American, material) which
will allow her to implement her plans.

I believe, however, that there is an easily overlooked lesson
to be learned here. Mrs. Kooi began with the local tradition,
invited all of her pupils to share in it (including her Asian pupils,
who are frequently asked to compare their acculturation expe-

riences to those of Pella's founders), and has then invited the pupils to learn about Dutch culture from a broader perspective. Obviously, the opposite approach also has its merits (*Hans Brinker* paves the way for *The Path of Delft*). In very general terms, however, I sense that it is more feasible, in Pella, to work from the local tradition into a broader understanding of Dutch culture than vice versa; such will, at any rate, almost certainly be the case as an ever-greater segment of Dutch culture makes its appearance in Pella and becomes a part of the local experience. The ideal, of course, would be synergism of "local" and "imported" forces.

Music Makes the Difference!

As Mr. Vander Leest pointed out in his Master's thesis, *Influence of the Holland Background on Education in the Pella Community Schools, 1847–1966*, music programs enjoy a long tradition in Pella of transmitting and enforcing an awareness of Dutch culture. In great part, this is due to the efforts of Miss Anne Tysseling, who took full advantage of the community's background, and opportunities provided by festivals such as Tulip Time. Miss Tysseling's resource materials have been passed on to Mrs. Brummel, who has amassed an enviable library of musical and cultural literature. In both the Community and Christian Schools, music plays a prominent role in heritage education: the entire year's program is infused with appropriate Dutch material, and that in a manner which clearly shows initiative on the instructor's part going beyond any mandated requirements; an astonishing passive (and at times even active) knowledge of the language is transmitted to pupils, with the result that music programs may be the unrecognized linch-pin in community efforts to revitalize language; the instructors themselves are remarkably versatile, and use the classroom (as observed in preparing this report) for instruction in Dutch geography, history and culture.

Mrs. Brummel has, in her quiet way, put into practice much of what others preach. A student of Jos Wuytack (a major figure in Dutch children's music), she has made a formal study of the Dutch language, has traveled to the Netherlands, where she gathered both general cultural material and a very full collection of children's musical literature, and has actively promoted ever-greater participation by the children of the Community Schools in festivals such a *Sinterklaas* and Tulip Time. She is also an outspoken proponent of greater interaction between her pupils and the community's older Dutch-American citizens.

During the school year, there is a steady flow of Dutch music. Thanksgiving and Pella's fall festival give opportunity for learning *Wilt heden nu treden* (the original of "We Gather Together") and various doxological literature. Christmas is marked by both secular and sacred songs. Spring brings its own genre of folksongs, and a birthday may well be marked by singing the Dutch *Lang zullen ze leven*. There are children's dances, songs with motions, and a sampling of international favorites (such as *Broeder Jacob*, or *Frère Jacques*). The musical selection may be the sweet lullaby *Slaap kindje slaap*, or a sober selection from the Dutch Psalter. A role model in all that she asks her children to do, Mrs. Brummel also performs, and her participation in recorder duets from the Psalter offers her pupils palpable inspiration.

Mr. Kooi, music teacher at Pella Christian Grade School, is also a person of many talents. In his "spare" time, he serves as the music director of a large Christian Reformed congregation, directs choral and bell-choir groups, and plays accordion for the Dutch Family Singers and Dancers. On the basis of classroom observation, I would have to conclude that he puts equal energy into an open and frank statement of his Christian principles, and in fact may see himself as much in the role of a spokesman for the faith as in that of a music instructor. In terms of the school's goals, as expressed by his principal, Mr. Groothuis, Mr. Kooi is probably just the sort of person needed in his position: a teacher of unquestioned credentials and talents; a member of the community sensitive to its values; an outspoken Christian in the Reformed tradition; that notwithstanding, an open-minded innovator.

The list of year-long features offered in Mr. Kooi's classes would, in great part, duplicate that given for Mrs. Brummel's classes. One difference, however, is worth dwelling upon, not because it represents any real divergence in the two instructors' outlooks, but rather in the areas chosen for emphasis in talks with the investigator.

Several informants (inter al., Mrs. Schiebout, Sr.) expressed the idea that of Pella's traditions which ought under no circumstances be allowed to founder is that of Dutch Psalm-singing. Mr. Kooi, who is active in revitalizing Psalm singing (and who has enjoyed some success in stirring up pupil interest) is seen by a number of persons as just the sort of influential figure required for a more-than-pro-forma perpetuation of this tradition. As I shall point out in the section on language learning, the real reason for language instruction is often not acquisition of fluency, but rather an approach to the affective and experiential domain of the older speakers (as Mrs. Zylstra said, to share in expression of the perspectives and feelings of those who have transmitted the heritage to us). In a similar vein, it is significant that Mr. Kooi found language instruction valuable in helping one to understand cultural origins or differences; an expression of complete range of human emotion, however (and hence, by contextual implication, the key to understanding ourselves), is given by the Dutch Psalter. Mr. Kooi has found, in the Dutch Psalter, the mechanism for addressing a fundamental issue in heritage education: the need to assure some sense of continuity between the constellation of emotional forces which sustained the older generation, and that which will motivate the up-coming generation.

Language Instruction

One frequently hears statements to the effect that Pella is down to her last 100 speakers of Dutch, and these are going fast! It is true that the primary speaker-population has now reached retirement age. I have engaged in free socialization in Dutch, however, with persons (n.b., not from the families of immigrants) who are as young as 30–35. This situation is admittedly a rare one, and I find it about the age-range of 50–55 which begins to offer an appreciable pool of speakers. As I have pointed out in some of my sociolinguistic studies, it is not so much the speaker of Dutch which is dying out, as is the sort of social situation which demanded its use.

It would be difficult to estimate the exact number of speakers, though if we are indeed down to our last 100, then I have observed, recorded or polled more speakers than are supposed to be available. Rather, such statements are to be seen as one reflection of the community's attitude toward the Dutch language. The Dutch spoken in Pella has a number of non-standard forms of which its speakers are acutely aware. In addition, the hybrid forms of the language in current use even by teenagers (Yankee Dutch) would not necessarily be intelligible to a person versed only in the standard language. There is probably no area of Dutch culture in which the difference between the "local" and the "imported" version is sensed as strongly as in the linguistic arena. It is policy *de rigeur* for a speaker approached by an investigator to delineate the difference between "High Dutch," *deftig* or *goed Hollands* (good Dutch) on the one hand, and "Low Dutch," "Pella Dutch" or "Household Dutch" on the other, and then (if one has not formally studied the language) to disclaim the status of a speaker. In one instance, a member of the community denied almost categorically any knowledge of the language, only later (admittedly, after a certain "thawing out" period) to give an interview, almost entirely in Dutch.

Two examples of non-standard forms might be given; both have, incidentally, been recorded among similar speaker-populations. One evening in my Dutch class at Central College a review of the Dutch verb *zijn* 'to be' (even more irregular in the present tense than its English equivalent) prompted a class member who is a prominent Pella resident, and quite clearly one for whom Dutch was a household language, to question the accuracy of my forms. He then gave the forms heard so frequently in Pella, which are perfectly regular, and based upon only one of the three stems used in the standard Dutch paradigm of the verb. Another hybrid form is *spraten* 'to talk.' Some see it as a blend of the synonyms *spreken* and *praten*; I have heard the incorrect syllabic division *Holland spraten* for *Hollands praten* 'to speak Dutch' so often that I prefer the latter as an explanation for the genesis of *spraten*.

At any rate, there is an unmistakable reticence exhibited by Pella's speakers of Dutch. For reasons alluded to above and for still other reasons too numerous to treat here, there is a long-standing aversion toward use of the language in the presence of "Americans," whose language is that of the dominant culture; there is an even greater hesitancy to use the language with any speaker of Dutch who might cast disparagement upon the local idiom. Ironically, it is precisely the abundance of non-standard forms in Pella Dutch which causes many speakers to despair of any hopes for the language's survival, and consequently to hasten its untimely demise through disuse, when, quite the contrary, the fact that such hybrid forms can evolve shows the linguist (who recognizes change as a universal of *living* languages) that Pella Dutch still exhibits the potential for vitality.

Several attempts have, in fact, been made to resuscitate Dutch in Pella. In the mid-1950s, one of the members of a prominent family approached the superintendent of the Community Schools, and persuaded him to initiate a Dutch program. The parent's son happened to be in the class of Miss Dena Versteeg, a teacher who, prior to her retirement in the early 1970's, dedicated over forty years of her life to public instruction; in addition to being a beloved and respected teacher, Miss Versteeg was—and continues to be—regarded as a precious human resource in our community for information on the local Dutch tradition. Fluent in Dutch, she approached the instruction of the language with a strong sense of concern for detail and correctness. I have had casual conversations with persons involved with her program, and all concur in giving it high marks, at least from the pupils' point of view. From the administrator's point of view, things were evidently less rosy. Scheduling adjustments needed to be made, especially for pupils who had begun as fifth-graders and wanted to continue as sixth-graders. At the end of the second year of the program, the principal intervened, and Dutch was dropped from the curriculum.

In 1978, Mrs. Harriet Zylstra, librarian and resources coordinator for the Pella Christian Grade School (which offers instruction through eighth grade) initiated an enrichment program in Dutch for seventh-graders. Classes met twice a week, and used a variety of materials. Mrs. Zylstra had obtained an instructional-materials grant from the Netherlands Ministry of Science and Education, which provided her with a complete course in Dutch. Although the Dutch materials were designed primarily for the younger children of guest workers in the Netherlands, Mrs. Zylstra adopted them to the needs of her pupils, produced a small handbook of conversational Dutch based on the everyday experiences of a traveler in the Netherlands, read from the New Testament in Today's Dutch (*Groot Nieuws voor U*), held memorization contests based on a locally produced and recently reprinted volume, *Dutch Nursery Rhymes*, and topped off the year with a Dutch meal, at which occasion one had to speak Dutch in order to be served.

It is worth noting that Mrs. Zylstra combined an appreciation for formal correctness in language instruction with a sensitivity to the potential of language as a transmitter of cultural values. Two points brought up in her interview might be cited to illustrate her views in this regard. On the one hand, her "wish list" (as well as that of her principal) would include the identification—and, if necessary, production—of a rigorous, challenging grammar suited to the needs of an American seventh grader, and geared toward helping the pupil in both languages. On the other hand, her real goal in teaching Dutch lies not so much in facilitating fluency, but rather in facilitating the participation of her pupils in the affective domain of their cultural forebearers, i.e., to "feel" like a Dutchman, and to be able to share those feelings in the one language which has proven itself capable of their expression.

(As an aside, one might mention the fact that "Yankee Dutch"—which is alive and doing very well, thank you, in the Pella Community and Christian Schools—consists primarily of English syntax and grammar with Dutch vocabulary; the overwhelming majority of "Yankee Dutch" terms express feelings or social activities for which English has no single term. Some examples are: *suf* 'dull, lethargic, unable to get moving'; *benauwd* 'constricted, stifled, oppressed, anxious'; *vies* 'squeemish, finicky, skittish'; *knoeien around* 'mess around, make a mess, bungle, botch up.' No doubt many of her pupils came to Mrs. Zylstra with at least some idea of how it felt to be a Dutchman.)

Considering that she did her work without special released time, Mrs. Zylstra certainly deserves the commendation which one hears from former pupils (and parents of the annual dozen or so pupils) associated with the Dutch program. By 1980, however, it was becoming clear that special scheduling considerations needed to be made, and hence, though the Christian Grade School remains proud as punch of the letters of praise which it received from the Dutch government, the program was dropped at the end of its second year. I believe that the Christian Grade School principal, Mr. Ivan Groothuis, is sincere in stating that the reintroduction of Dutch would be a priority for any future program revisions; time alone will tell if such is to be the case.

Still another program was tried out in the late 1960's with the combined seventh and eighth graders at the Christian School in nearby Peoria, Iowa (a community strongly identified with the Dutch-American territory surrounding Pella). Mr. Robert De Jager, a native of the Netherlands and principal-teacher of the seventh/eighth grade class, introduced Dutch, only to find that, in time, parents complained that pupils were putting too much energy into Dutch at the expense of other subjects, and that some seventh-grade pupils felt disadvantaged being in the same class with eighth-graders who had studied Dutch the year before. Scheduling and feasibility problems became apparent, and, in a now hauntingly familiar pattern, the program was dropped at the end of its second year.

Mr. De Jager, however, is both versatile and resiliant. Upon retirement (and a feature article in the local newspaper on his many-sided career), this educator-broadcaster-musician-preacher-craftsman moved to Pella. Here he immersed himself even more fully than before in church and civic activities, in his weekly Dutch-language radio program, and in a variety of educational programs, particularly those of the Christian Opportunity Center (a special-education and sheltered workshop complex).

At the same time, Mr. De Jager quietly began tutoring Dutch. Without any particular advertisement, he has worked (since autumn, 1981) with six pupils from four families. Some measure of his success is given by the fact that all of his pupils but one are continuing through the summer, and that two high-school age pupils (one who had dropped out of the program because of a heavy schedule of sports and studies, and another who had been in Mrs. Zylstra's program) have voluntarily reinitiated their study of Dutch under Mr. De Jager. Parents appear to be more than satisfied with the instructor, whose lesson typically includes not only grammar and useful expressions, but also some religious text (a prayer, a verse from the Dutch Psalter, the retelling of a Bible story, or the text of a hymn). The latter reflects the point made by Mr. De Jager during his interview, that one of the most useful aspects of language study in his own experience has been the ability it has given him to get at the core meaning of Scripture by comparing the way in which the same idea is expressed in several languages. Although it was said in the context of his ability to relate well across generational lines, I sense that the concern for the understanding and transmission of religious values was also implied in the statement of one parent that the instructor is "the sort of person every child should experience at least once."

The reasons that pupils give for learning Dutch differ little from those given by pupils in similar programs elsewhere: there is a desire to socialize with members of the older generation, to come closer to one's roots, and to be prepared for a more meaningful travel experience in the Netherlands. Even though there is little activity in realization of these goals, both pupils and parents seem remarkably content with the results of the language programs. I strongly suspect that language fluency per se is not the real objective of language classes. Rather, participation in the classes is seen as a sign of affirmation of values which must now be transmitted to the coming generation. Mrs. Schiebout, Sr., who is delighted with her granddaughters' language studies, was quite clear in stating that what she wanted most for her grandchildren was the perpetuation of the religious experience and a love of cleanliness (cf. comments above on community values!). This does not mean that she is indifferent to the language: much of our interview centered around the "untranslatables" of the Dutch language. It simply means that cultural components (such as the language) are merely reflections of cultural values.

Another example of language-learning as affirmation of group values was given by Mr. Gosselink, who spoke at length of the need for a special tie to, and respect for, the Dutch heritage. During his time in the military service, Mr. Gosselink met members of another Dutch-American community; while he was delighted to be able to communicate with his ethnic peers, he regretted the fact that they were generally more fluent in Dutch than he, and hence perhaps a bit closer to the generation which was more fully Dutch. Without being particularly adament on the point, he hopes that language instruction will give his children a chance to realize what he would have wanted to experience.

Among the factors cited for giving one child Dutch lessons was the fact that she reportedly cried to learn that she was only half Dutch-American. The child had already made the first statement of affirmed solidarity with the ethnic group, and should therefore be allowed to make the next logical step in affirming its heritage and values. The point, of course, is not the charming story of the child, but rather the insight which it gives us into community attitudes. Among other things, ethnic heritage education becomes part of a rite of passage, and the failure to recognize it as such and support it for its underlying value would, as the extreme consequence, mean a deterioration of the ties which contribute to group cohesiveness across generational lines.

Assessments and Projections

It may well be that the future of heritage and language education will lie to an ever-greater extent outside of formal school settings. In addition to private language tutoring, there are several private and public programs which may assume more and more importance. The Dutch Family Singers and Dancers are a cooperative venture by a number of families (and individuals) who practice Dutch songs and dances to be performed at Tulip Time and on various occasions throughout the year. Most recently, a small contingent performed at the send-off ceremony for three students who had won free trips to the Netherlands in an essay contest sponsored by the Pella Historical Society. Several years ago, the group traveled to Ames, Iowa to welcome the (overwhelmed) members of the visiting Amsterdam Concertgebouw Orchestra. The group has been active for nearly twenty years, and counts among its members senior citizens, children whose parents are not members, but who come with friends whose families are, singles, couples, and entire families. Practice sessions for the group are the only occasion on which I have observed or experienced spontaneous socialization in Dutch with persons my age (mid- to late 30's). While it is not overwhelmingly common, some join the group for the express purpose of exposing their children to other persons who use the Dutch language. Such was the case, for example, for the family of an active member of the Christian Reformed Church and a leader in the Calvinist Cadet Core (Christian Reformed scout program). Though only in his early 30's, the father of the family is an active speaker of Dutch who consistently greets me in both languages. A program began this year at the public library which includes a component of Dutch children's lore, nursery rhymes, sayings in Dutch, and Dutch children's literature in translation.

The idea which holds the most promise is that of instituting a "Board of Dutch Education" in Pella. It is envisioned that such a group would be influential in the coordination and centralization of efforts such as those described here, and would address itself to matters of feasibility and follow-through in those instances where an instructor or program director needs energy and/or sheer influence which goes beyond her/his own resources. The head of such a group would have to be an individual (or governing committee) with considerable credibility and influence, and, above all, the ability to bring together the community's many interests without favor or partiality. I sincerely wish Pella the realization of such hopes, and that with as little delay as possible.

[The original Report was followed by a Select Bibliography, omitted here because virtually all items are already cited in the notes and Bibliography of this volume.]

NOTES

Part One

1. This information may be extrapolated from the data presented in a report culled from 1980 census data: *Ancestry of the Population by State: 1980* (Washington, D.C.: GPO, 1983). This information was brought to public attention by David Westphal, "Diversely Ethnic Iowa No. 1 in Dutch Ancestry," *Des Moines Sunday Register* for July 7, 1985. Also of interest to ethno-sociolinguists is *Ancestry and Language in the United States: November, 1979* (Washington, D.C.: GPO, 1982).
2. There is no single definitive history of Pella, though several works merit the attention of serious scholars.

   For general background on the Dutch in America, see Swierenga, "Dutch," 284–95, and Lucas, *Netherlanders in America*. For Iowa, one must at some point refer to the older but still valuable work of Van der Zee, *The Hollanders in Iowa*. For a Dutchman's assessment, as well as previously unstudied and understudied source material, one might turn to J. Stellingwerff, *Amsterdamse Emigranten. Onbekende Brieven uit de Prairie van Iowa. 1846–1873* (Amsterdam: Buijten and Schipperheijn, 1975). A work more comprehensive in scope, whose English version appeared only as this document was being completed, is Van Hinte, *Netherlanders in America*. The earlier Dutch edition is virtually unavailable to the general scholar in this country. Also too recent to receive thorough treatment was Swierenga, *The Dutch in America*.

   The earliest serious attempt at a systematic history of Pella by a locally based author was Van Stigt, *Geschiedenis van Pella, Iowa en Omgeving*. This was followed by the more widely read Stout, *Souvenir History of Pella, Iowa*. For Scholte and the religious movement that brought him to Pella, one might wish to consult

Oostendorp, *H. P. Scholte;* for in-depth research, there is a wealth of source material in Smit, *De Afscheiding van 1834,* especially vols. 3, 5 and 6. For the specific migration that resulted in the settlement at Pella, see the Leiden doctoral dissertation by Stokvis, *De Nederlandse trek naar Amerika, 1846–1847.* For one of the most thought-provoking studies to appear in recent years, which treats Pella from a different perspective, see Doyle, *The Socio-Economic Mobility of the Dutch Immigrants to Pella, Iowa 1847–1925,* with a summary in Swierenga, *The Dutch in America,* 156–71.

I wish to thank Prof. Raymond Den Adel for his faithful sharing of research on the many communities throughout the world that bear the name Pella.

Although a fictionalized account that in no way is confined to Pella, one might turn to P. J. Risseuw's triology *Landverhuizers* (Baarn: Bosch and Keuning, 1962).

3. Among the various accounts of life in Pella to appear in the popular press, one might note: Rouché, "Profiles: Oasis," 46–68, and again in somewhat different form in Rouché, *Special Places,* 155–87; Teddern, "Another Netherlands," 20–26; *A Historic Guide to Pella;* Van Klompenburg, "Time out for Tulips," 4–13.

In 1982, an architectural walking tour of Pella was planned, and a permanent slide-tape show placed on deposit at the Pella Historical Society. The tour, described on the centerfold of the *Historic Guide,* was designed by Humanist-in-Residence Philip E. Webber, under a grant from the Iowa Humanities Board/National Endowment for the Humanities. For background on Pella's architectural *notabilia,* see the articles by Muriel Byers Kooi in *The Iowan* for December-January (1960–61): 30–37 and 50; fall (1973): 4–11; spring (1974): 12–14; summer (1975): 46–51.

For other aspects of Pella's folk heritage as expressed in art and crafts, see Webber, "Everyday Elaborations: Three Traditional Iowa Communities," 90–101.

The Pella Historical Society is currently compiling a two-volume anthology of short articles on local and family history.

For a brief comparison of Pella and the Flemish-American community at Victor, Iowa, see Webber, "Nederlanders en Vlamingen in Iowa," 458–60.

4. Among the varied reactions of native Dutchmen to Pella's ethnic self-celebration, see Van Deutekom, "Het Rijke Reformatorische Leven in Pella, Iowa," 69–74.

5. I am indebted to Prof. W. J. Vande Kopple of Calvin College for sharing some of his unpublished studies on the impact of Dutch on the English in areas of strong ethnic concentration. Little has appeared in print on the subject since Veltman, "Dutch Survivals in Holland, Michigan," 80–83, and Vander Werff, "Evidence of Old Holland in the Speech of Grand Rapids," 301–4. To these specifically linguistic studies might be added the observations of Lucas, *Netherlanders in America,* 585.

For work bearing directly on the language of Dutch immigrants and their descendants in Pella, see Daan, "Bilingualism of Dutch Immigrants in the U.S.A.," *Actes* 759–63, and (with the same title) *Dichtung.* 205–13; "Verschuiven van isoglossen," 77–80; more generally, Daan, "Language Use and Language Policy among Americans of Dutch Origin," 207–17. An interesting reaction by local residents to this earlier work on immigrant language is given in the article "Dutch Dialect Studies Completed. More Dutch Here Than Other Areas," *Pella Chronicle* for October 18, 1966. Cf. the note by Webber and Davis, "Bericht. Pella Dutch: Mogelijkheden voor Sociolinguïstisch Onderzoek," 83–84. Dr. Jo Daan shared data from her recently published book-length study on Dutch spoken abroad. Several interviews conducted in Pella in the 1960s are cited in her work.

6. Mr. Buerkens' articles in the *Pella Chronicle* for August 8 and August 15, 1979, were based on texts considered locally to be the finest of Yankee Dutch anthologies: Lieuwen, *Sweat and Tears.* Less commonly cited, but perhaps even more valuable, is Nieland, *'n fonnie bisnis.* The parallel vocabulary of English, Yankee Dutch, and Dutch terms gives a fairly comprehensive overview of Yankee Dutch's hybrid lexicon.

7. For examples of attempts to engage in just such changes of a distinctly ethnic family name, see Lucas *Netherlanders in America,* 583.

8. I am deeply indebted to Mrs. Sarah Caldwell for sharing the fruits of her personal research on the topic, much of which has been verified by collateral evidence from interviews and personal memoirs.

9. Dorian, *Language Death.*

10. Cf. ibid., 160, where Dorian notes, as must eventually each responsible field investigator: "Despite the shortcomings just discussed in the responses to [one of the questionnaires], I am relatively comfortable in presenting its results precisely because I have

sufficient experience to interpret them and to contradict them where necessary."

11. James Dow, "Deutsch als Muttersprache in Iowa." In *Deutsch als Muttersprache in den Vereinigten Staaten, Teil I: Der Mittelwesten* edited by Leopold Auburger, Heing Kloss and Heing Rupp, (Wiesbaden: Franz Steiner, 1979), 91–118.

　　For a summary of his previous work, see Lawrence L. Rettig, *Amana Today: A History of the Amana Colonies From 1932 to the Present*, privately published by the author, n.d. [1975], 101–9; for greater depth see his 1967 M.A. thesis at University of Iowa, "Segmental Phonemes of the Amana Dialect," his 1970 Ph.D. dissertation for the same institution, "Grammatical Structures in Amana German," and "Amana German Anew," *American Speech* 44 (1969): 55–66.

　　Studies of a number of linguistic groups and communities in the Midwest are given in Schach, *Languages in Conflict*.

12. Much of the inspiration for this kind of informant selection comes from Wolfgang Wölck, "Community Profiles: An Alternative Approach to Linguistic Informant Selection," 43–57. While Michael D. Linn may present valid considerations concerning such methods for dialect research in his study "Informant Selection in Dialectology," *American Speech* 58/3(1983): 225–43, the establishment of a community profile for informants nevertheless remains a technique ideally suited for certain types of sociolinguistic investigation.

13. The Dutch-American settlements of Northwest Iowa were originally offshoots of the Pella settlement. Cf. Lucas, *Netherlanders in America*, 330–58, and Van der Zee, *The Hollanders in Iowa*, 122 ff. and passim. Depending whom one asks, Pella either enjoys a head start because of its greater number of years as an established center of Dutch-American culture in the Midwest, or merits the distinction of having had the greater amount of time in which to depart from its heritage. It is true that Dutch seems to be somewhat more readily spoken in the younger colonies of Northwest Iowa, though I shall leave to others the formulation of any evaluative statements about what this may mean about the "Dutchness" of the various communities.

14. In general, the patterns of migration, in terms of region of origin, correspond to those suggested by Swierenga, "Exodus Netherlands, Promised Land America," 127–47, and Stokvis, *De Nederlandse trek naar Amerika*, 5, 13.

15. For five years I conducted a survey on self-image and ethnicity as part of the work for my course Ethnic Groups in Iowa, taught at

Central College in Pella, Iowa. Denial or at least downplaying of a Dutch background appeared to be a constant for approximately 5–10% of those surveyed in the years 1977–1981.

16. A report on language education in Pella was completed by Philip E. Webber as part of the Ethnic Heritage and Language Schools project of the American Folklife Center of the Library of Congress in 1982. The report appears as Appendix B of the present work. Interim reports on the project appeared in the *Folklife Center News* for January and July, 1982. For a general history of the schools in Pella, see Emma Lou Heusinkveld, *Pella School History, 1847–1980* (Pella: Pella Printing Co., 1980); it is also worthwhile comparing the field data gathered by Merlyn Vander Leest for his 1966 Master of Science in Education thesis at Drake University, "Influence of the Holland Background on Education in the Pella Community Schools, 1847–1966."

17. In the concluding seminar of fieldworkers who had participated in the Ethnic Heritage and Language Schools project (see note 16), it was repeatedly stressed by investigators working within highly divergent settings that the purpose of language education (like the use of Dutch on special occasions in Pella) is less for reasons of actual cross-generational communication of specific ideas or facts and more a means of affirming continuity in the face of pressure to assimilate (i.e., to melt within the pot).

18. Similar phenomena have been reported in many settings, perhaps most recently at a conference on Dutch in emigrant communities, held in July, 1984, at the Meertens Institute in Amsterdam, and reported inter al. in *NRC Handelsblad* for July 7, 1984. I am indebted to colleagues in Amsterdam for supplying me with summaries of the papers presented.

19. For details, see the report cited in note 16.

Part Two

1. The motto is that of the Reformed Church in America (and also, incidentally, of the nation of Belgium). It enjoys a local response among a certain group of speakers as a call to unity; as late as 1917

it was used by the Pella High School basketball team (printed on banners in the unwittingly garbled form *Een Dracht Maakt Macht* [a costume makes power]) when the players went to the state tournament, as can clearly be seen in photos on display at the Pella Community Center.

There is a certain wisdom to the Dutch joke, applicable to areas of life other than just religion, that with one Dutchman there will be a religion, with two Dutchmen a denomination, and with three Dutchmen a schism. Dutchmen display a tendency to seek a group of those like themselves, but then to keep that group separate from others of even only slightly different persuasions or backgrounds. Cf. note 3.

2. Data on what is considered to be Dutch-American territory surrounding Pella was first gathered in 1977–79 by members of my course on Ethnic Groups in Iowa. I have since regularly polled informants on this point, and here present those opinions on which there was consensus, if not in fact unanimity. See also the literature cited in note 55.

3. Perhaps the best short treatment of this point is that by Swierenga, *The Dutch in America*, 15–42. Cf. the maps and literature cited by Swierenga, "Exodus Netherlands, Promised Land America," 127–47. Less commonly cited, but more voluminous in scope, is Petersen, *Planned Migration*.

4. This is a point for which I am still seeking reasonably compelling evidence from the period of settlement. Virtually all sources who admit having given the matter any thought, however, do subscribe to the view presented here. The theory that Dutchmen tried to replicate the topography of their home region in the Netherlands was itself first presented to me by local residents.

For an account of clustering by region of origin in an urban setting, see David G. Vanderstel, "Dutch Immigrant Neighborhood Development in Grand Rapids, 1850–1900," in Swierenga, *The Dutch in America*, 125–55.

5. For now, the best overview of the history of Tulip Time is Kooi, *Festival*. The exact role of the early picnics is still open to debate.

6. "Herwyner's [sic] Have a Jolly Time," *The Pella Press*, August 27, 1930.

7. Ibid.

8. Ibid. I am particularly grateful to those individuals who shared personal diary entries concerning the picnic and its featured events.

9. This, unfortunately, is a point of near unanimity in the recollections of many speakers. Few, however, can really say just who is

actually supposed to have profited through any (allegedly) unabashed opportunism.

10. "Herwyner's [sic] Have a Jolly Time."
11. Ibid.
12. See Wabeke, *Dutch Emigration to North America 1624–1860*, 121, 131 [where a facsimile is given of the 1847 Baltimore *Sun* article describing the landing of Scholte's band], and the sources that he cites. There is no question that Iowa welcomed the Dutchmen, as it did so many immigrants at that time: see, for instance *IOWA: The Home For Immigrants* [with a Dutch edition entitled] *Iowa: Het Land voor Emigranten* (Iowa City: The State Historical Society of Iowa, 1970), reprint of the original 1870 English edition, with facsimile title pages from the German and Dutch editions.
13. Lucas, *Netherlanders in America*, 191–92, with further documentation cited. Scholte believed that even those who could not or would not vote were influential through their presence at moments of decision making: see, for instance, H. P. Scholte, *Tweede Stem uit Pella* ('s-Hertogenbosch: H. Parlier and Son, 1848), 12.
14. On the mutual admiration of Lincoln, Scholte, and Michigan's Van Raalte, see Mulder, *Americans from Holland*, 140, 244. In all of his writings, Scholte came forth squarely in favor of Lincoln, who at one point had hoped to appoint Scholte ambassador to Austria. There is evidence to suggest that the admiration for Lincoln among Dutch-Americans continued for some time. One of the more popular pieces of patriotic literature in Pella during the first years of this century was Henry Beets, *Abraham Lincoln. zijn tijd en leven* (Grand Rapids, Michigan: J. B. Hulst and B. Sevensma, 1909). See also note 15.
15. Lucas, *Netherlanders in America*, 591. Scholte published the first antislavery tract to appear west of the Mississippi, *American Slavery, in Reference to the Present Agitation of the United States. By an Adopted Citizen* (Pella: Gazette Book and Job Office, 1856).
16. Scholte is adamant on this point in the opening essay to the second (and final) volume of the Messianic and eschatological series *De Toekomst* (Pella: Henry Hospers, 1868), 1–3, noting near the end of the piece that "in Christus [is] niet Dutch, German, or [sic] American" (in Christ there is neither Dutch, German or American).
17. See Scholte's visionary editorial on Pella's future in the *Pella Gazette* for February 1, 1855. In the same issue, Scholte notes conspicuously on the front page that through his efforts a petition had been made two years earlier to locate the state capitol in Pella.
18. For a vignette on education in both languages in the schools in and

around Pella, see Nollen, *De Hollanders in Iowa*, 125. Only the most tantalizingly brief data appeared in the section "Elementary Instruction," in Van Stigt, *History of Pella and Vicinity*, 82–83. Commenting on the situation in the Christian schools in Dutch communities, Lucas *Netherlanders in America*, 601–2, notes that "the chief concern . . . until the 1880s was the teaching of the Dutch language."

19. Cited by Lucas, *Netherlanders in America*, 590.
20. One of the best treatments of the course that such shame takes is given by Andrew M. Greeley in "Steps in Ethnic Assimilation," in his *Why Can't They Be Like Us? America's White Ethnic Groups* (New York: E. P. Dutton, 1971), 53–59. Greeley sees six steps in the acculturation process: 1. cultural shock; 2. organization and emergent self-consciousness; 3. assimilation of the elite; 4. militancy; 5. self-hatred and antimilitancy; 6. emerging adjustment. One local wag claims that Pella and certain other communities have taken a seventh step: commercial exploitation of the ethnic heritage.
21. *De Sheboygan Nieuwsbode* for March 14, 1854, cited by Lucas, *Netherlanders in America*, 608–9.
22. For an overview of Dutch-American journalism, see Bult, "Dutch-American Newspapers: Their History and Role," in *Swieringa, The Dutch in America*, 273–93. It was not possible to consult Hendrik Edelman, *The Dutch Language Press in America* (Nieuwkoop, The Netherlands: De Graaf, 1986), that appeared after conclusion of work on the present volume.

    It should be noted at the outset, however, that Pella's situation was not entirely typical for that of the Dutch-American press in general. Mulder notes in *Americans from Holland*, 238, that as a rule (presumably in Calvinistic communities?) "questions of doctrine were much more real to [a newspaper's] readers than secular political issues." Even the most cursory survey of Pella's weekly newspapers shows that doctrinal debates seldom dominated any single issue, and certainly never set the long-range tone for any of the town's regular publications.

    It also needs to be stressed that the earlier Pella papers, such as the *Weekblad* (from which many learned to read Dutch), were unabashedly frolicsome in tone, and full of admissions, such as the tongue-in-cheek disclaimer at the end of a bit of forcefully rhymed word-play doggerel published on December 22, 1899, that the material printed need not be mistaken for that of any great Dutch literary figure: "Wat zoudt gij rijmen op een podding? vroeg eens iemand en antwoord[d]e zelf daarop 'Een houten lepel is een pot-ding / Een zachte mispel is een rot-ding / Een uitgestoken tong is een spot-ding / Een uitgelaten lach is een zot-ding.' " ('What rhymes with pudding?' someone asked, and then answered himself: 'A wooden spoon is a pot-thing [Dutch: *pot-ding*, cf. *podding* 'pudding'] / A soft piece of fruit is a rot-thing [*rot-ding*] / A tongue stuck out is a derisive thing [*spot-ding*] / An uncontrolled laugh is a dumb thing [*zot-ding*].') True, the paper did publish an occasional timely poem by a notable literary figure (on December 1, 1916, for example, by Ten Kate, on war) or a well-known proverb (e.g., "Het geld, dat stom is / Maakt recht, wat krom is" [money, though silent, can make the crooked straight]), November 10, 1899. Already by February 23, 1900, however, the paper was plagued by a lack of workers who were fluent in Dutch: the foreman of the printing operation, though lauded by the publisher as industrious and well meaning, knew only English. In a very literal sense, by the time that any of today's living informants made their acquaintance with it, Dutch journalism was in the hands of the Americans.

23. "En daarom zal Pella immer blijven wat het is: een langzaam bloeiend, maar welvarend landstadje . . . waar de farmers op gezette tijd hun inkopen komen doen . . . maar groot, een stad van handel en beweging en fabrieken zal Pella nooit worden (en dat willen wij ook liever niet)." *Weekblad* for May 3, 1901.

24. The *Groentje* is by no means a Pella phenomenon: see, for example, Mulder, *Americans from Holland*, 247.

25. Cf. Lucas, *Netherlanders in America*, 594–97; Mulder, *Americans from Holland*, 265–73.

26. I am indebted to Jayne Gaunt for first pointing out the editorial essays by Solano.

27. In the journalist's own words: "Ons wordt verweten dat wij te veel Nederlandsch gezind zijn, dat wij bedenken moeten dat wij thans Amerikanen zijn"; in an article celebrating the marriage of Her Majesty Queen Wilhelmina, *Weekblad* for February 8, 1901.

28. In an editorial "Iets over Nederland en Amerika," *Weeekblad* for December 14, 1900, Solano claims: "Het wordt hier hoe langer meer de gewoonte voor kinderen van Hollandsche ouders om beschaamd te zijn voor hunne afkomst. Zij schamen zich werkelijk . . .dat ze Hollandsch bloed in de aderen hebben . . . en, als zodanig, is het geen wonder dat zij Amerikansiche toestanden toejuichen, dat ze meer Amerikaan zijn dan de Amerikaan zelf." (The longer it goes, the more customary it becomes for the children of Dutch parents to be ashamed of their origin. They are truly

ashamed . . . that they have Dutch blood in their veins . . . and as such it is no wonder that they affirm the American way, and that they are more American than the Americans themselves.)

29. Keizer, "De Nederlandsche Taal in Amerika," 503–5. Keizer concludes with a concession to the inevitability of dominance by the American language: "Men moge onze moedertaal zoolang mogelijk vasthouden. Hiernaar streve onze bond! Maar,—God geeft elk volk zijn eigen taal en de taal der toekomst is de taal van dit land: de *Amerikaaansche* taal! *Ik heb gezegd.* [P.S. 'Ik beek je pardon' dat ik van den winter in den zomer gevallen ben, n.l. met mijn 'speech!' . . . 'Excuse me.' 'Certainly!']" (May we hold onto our Dutch language as long as possible. That is what our organization is working for! But . . . God gives each people its own language, and the language of the future is the language of this country: the *American* language! *I have spoken.* [P.S. 'I beg your pardon' (a play on words in the Dutch) that I jumped from winter to summer in my 'speech!' . . . 'Excuse me.' 'Certainly!'])

    It is interesting to compare this with the unsigned front-page editorial in the *Weekblad* for September 9, 1901, where it is clear that the battle over language was indeed raging, but also that those observing it took a curiously ambivalent stand.

30. The term schizoglossia has gained currency in great part through Einar Haugen's "Schizoglossia and the Linguistic Norm," in Haugen, *The Ecology of Language,* 148–54.

31. *Weekblad* for October 20, 1899.

32. Ibid., December 22, 1899.

33. Ibid., November 10, 1899.

34. On the notion that Dutch was somehow a "more religious language," see Mulder, *Americans from Holland,* 245, 248.

35. "De Zaterdagavond in Pella," *Weekblad* for September 15, 1899.

36. Ibid., February 21, 1902.

37. For the ad, see, for example, the *Weekblad* for August 13, 1915; on Central College's Reformed Church affiliation, ibid., June 16, 1916, in the same newpaper for June 30, 1916, we read "Prof. [H. J.] Brouwer is een lid van de Ger[eformeerde] kerk en komt van een goede Hollandsche familie af, en spreekt even goed Hollandsch als Engelsch." (Prof. [H. J.] Brouwer is a member of the [Christian] Reformed Church, comes from a good Dutch family, and speaks just as good Dutch as English.)

38. Doyle, *The Socio-Economic Mobility of the Dutch Immigrants to Pella, Iowa 1847–1925,* 123, 127.

39. Swierenga, "Exodus Netherlands," 144.

40. Preface to a front-page ad appearing inter al. in *Pella's Nieuwsblad* for February 1, 1901; the ad was frequently repeated.
41. See the *Weekblad* for February 8–29, and especially for February 29.
42. E.g., *Weekblad* for October 6, 1899, and especially for December 3, 1899. On Pella's staunch record as supporters of the Democratic party, see Anthony Gene Carey, *Apocalyptic Vision and Political Oppression: The Origins of the Politics of the Pella Dutch*, Senior Honors Thesis (Pella: Central College, 1983).
43. *Weekblad* for December 1, 1916.
44. See especially the *Weekblad* May 25 through June 15, 1917.
45. Appears, inter al., in a front page ad in the *Weekblad* for October 19, 1917. On the bond sales and generally on ethnic groups in the face of emerging linguistic and xenophobic paranoia, see Derr, "The Babel Proclamation," 98–115.
46. See the *Weekblad* for February 9 and 23, 1917, and for February 22, 1918; cf. also note 14.
47. *Weekblad* for November 3, 1916. In the words of journalist: "Hij bedekt veel waarheid. Hij stelde zijn zijde voor op een slimme manier, en voor den man die niet beter wist of voor zichzelve denkt maakte hij een goed adres. Zijn gehele rede was er op aangelegd zijn hoorders te behagen en toch niets te zeggen dat veel betekenis had."
48. Derr, "Babel Proclamation," 107.
49. *Weekblad* for November 10, 1916.
50. Derr, "Babel Proclamation," 106, 111; for general background on such actions, see Frederick C. Luebke, "Legal Restrictions on Foreign Languages in the Great Plains States, 1917–1923," in Schach, *Languages in Conflict*, 1–19.
51. Quoted by Derr, "Babel Proclamation," 114.
52. *Weekblad* for May 18, 1917.
53. *Weekblad* for October 14, 1917; cf. Derr, "Babel Proclamation," 104.
54. Derr, "Babel Proclamation," 109; cf. *Weekblad* for May 31 through June 21, 1918.
55. The front page of the *Pella Chronicle* for June 20, 1918, featured a number of interesting articles, including one on ministers in Sully and Bethel accused of flouting the governor's language edict, and another on the conflagration of a church and parochial school in Peoria, where a pastor had recently been "forced to leave on account of the wrath of his neighbors at his lack of patriotic support of the government in the war." The parochial school, which burned

to the ground, had also been "a point of contension [*sic*] in the neighborhood because of its attitude toward American institutions and the implied contempt of its supporters for the public school." For an account of Peoria's conflicts, see Dahm and Van Kooten, *Peoria, Iowa*, 56–77.

56. Derr, "Babel Proclamation," 115; on the inability of other Dutch (i.e., those in Grand Rapids, Michigan) to unite and mobilize themselves politically, see Lucas, *Netherlanders in America*, 574.
57. Lucas, *Netherlanders in America*, 597.
58. On the use of catechetical texts in language instruction, see Lucas, *Netherlanders in America*, 590, 597.
59. The source in question did have paternal grandparents in the Reformed Church, but she and others affirm that it was a desire to build language skills, as much or more than a desire to please relatives, that led to attendance at the catechism classes.
60. J. Ellerbroek, in his series "Amerikanisatie. Enige Gedachte," *Weekblad* for February 23, 1923. For an excellent introduction to the broader issues of acculturation, see Bratt, "The Reformed Churches and Acculturation," and his more extensive *Dutch Calvinism in Modern America*. For specifically religious issues, see Bruins, "Americanization in Reformed Religious Life," and his case study, *The Americanization of a Congregation*.
61. The Central College *Pelican*, published by the Juniors of Central College, 13 (1921): 80.
62. It was lack of personnel and of younger editorial staff, rather than wartime conditions per se, that closed down the *Weekblad:* see H. L. Boland's parting note in the *Weekblad* for December 31, 1942.

Part Three

1. The point of reference in determining what is to be regarded as standard Dutch grammar is the monumental *Algemene Nederlandse Spraakkunst* edited by G. Geerts, et al. (Groningen: Wolters-Noordhoff; Louvain: Wolters, 1984). For the sounds of Dutch, Collins and Mees, *The Sounds of Dutch and English*, is particularly helpful. Though intended for Dutch-speaking students

of English, the work covers a clear contrastive overview for comparativists working at many levels.

I would note that even the most careful works do not hesitate to use standard Dutch orthographic conventions to cite variant forms, including those that serve as basic data for dialect studies (see also the work by Jo Daan and D. P. Blok cited in note 12). I have, therefore, felt it appropriate to use Dutch spelling whenever feasible to render the forms of Pella Dutch.

2. Nancy C. Dorian, in *Language Death*, 109 and note 27. Dorian's observations are based on fieldwork among speakers of Gaelic and Pennsylvania German.

3. This fact is borne out by the number of speakers who either made no effort to teach their children Dutch, or who in fact tried to avoid doing so, and yet found that a child with the personality type described managed to acquire the language, often with remarkable skill. One informant, who allowed his children to chart their own linguistic course in life, takes delight in telling how an especially outgoing son who served in the Navy simply approached a Dutch seaman with "Hoe is't ermee?" (How is it going?) and struck up a spontaneous conversation. Examples could be multiplied to show that the overwhelming majority of "final speakers" were as much motivated by an internal drive to social interaction as by any external pressures.

4. Virtually all of the rhymes that one encounters can be found in *Dutch Nursery Rhymes*, compiled by Elisabeth Kempkes and illustrated by Wilma Hadley (Pella: Pella's Weekblad, 1939, reprinted 1979 by the Tulip City Golden Agers). Obviously, the rhymes are subject to variations in their transmission and retelling, and for the first two examples cited I have given versions that vary from Kempke's text. Any number of rhymes were cited in part (or, at my suggestion, in their entirety); these two, however, were recited without any prompting on my part, and are therefore spontaneous, and not an attempt to give a "correct rendering."

5. In working with the data of this and the following section, one must bear in mind that it is often difficult to make an absolute distinction between essentially Dutch forms that may show some influence from English and Dutch forms that perpetuate a feature that was possible in an earlier stage of the language or would be plausible enough in a particular region of the Netherlands. In section 5 of her recently published study on Dutch outside the Netherlands, Dr. Jo Daan treated several such items in greater detail than is feasible in this context.

6. On *wezen* and its usage in Dutch, see inter al. Jo Daan's brief but thought-provoking " 'Zijn'-kultuur moet niet wezen," *Taal en Tongval* 39 (1987): 95–96.

7. Cf. A. van Loey, *Schönfelds Historische Grammatica van het Nederlands*, rev. ed. (Zutphen: W. J. Thieme, 1964), par. 147 c, note.

8. Though much augmented by subsequent literature, the standard study on *er* remains Gunnar Bech, *Über das niederländische Adverbialpronomen er*, Travaux du Cercle Linguistique de Copenhague 8 (Copenhagen: Nordisk Sprog- og Kulturforlag; Amsterdam: Taalinstituut De Natuurmethode, 1952).

9. The typical designation of a Dutch dialect consists of the name of the area in which it predominates (minus any inflectional ending or added compounding elements), with *-s* added (e.g., Utrechts, Herwijns, Gelders). See also notes 1 and 12.

10. This may be true, though my own suspicion is that in former times there simply was a greater number of speakers, with more representatives of each dialect, and hence the odds were greater that one might detect regionalisms without special effort, during the course of day-to-day conversations. I cannot honestly say that I find younger speakers less prone than older ones toward using forms characteristic of a particular area in the Netherlands.

11. On the occurrence of forms such as the one noted here, see Klaas Heeroma, *Taalatlas van Oost-Nederland en aangrenzende gebieden* (Assen: Van Gorcum, 1957), the map for *wren*. The vowel of the third syllable in *toenekriepertjie* is unusual in being unrounded, and one wonders whether this is exactly the form once used, or the form as recalled some years later.

12. When not otherwise stated, I have based the identification of dialect forms on the compact but very useful Daan and Blok, *Van Randstad tot Landrand*. Throughout this section, however, my first principle has been to be descriptive, so that colleagues with greater interest and expertise in dialects per se can determine whether they wish to pursue the study of dialect vestiges in Pella.

13. The standard study on the dialect of Utrecht, and the reference point for my own observations on traces of this dialect, is Van Veen, *Utrecht tussen oost en west*. I have also referred to Daan and Heeroma, *Zuidhollands*.

14. On the confusion of *liggen* and *leggen*, see K. Heeroma, *Hollandse dialektstudies*, map 4 and commentary, 13 f.; A. Weijnen, *Nederlandse dialectkunde*, 2d ed. (Assen: Van Gorcum, 1966), map 33.

15. Although *zijde* contains in its final syllable the trace of an assimilated enclitic pronoun *ge*, the form virtually never occurs in Pella

Dutch without a following (historically redundant) *ge.*

16. The standard treatment of such variant forms is G. G. Kloeke, *Een oud sjibboleth: De gewestelijke uitspraak van "heeft",* Verhandelingen der Koninklijke Nederlandse Akademie van Wetenschappen, Afdeling Letterkunde, new series, vol. 43, part 1 (Amsterdam: North Holland, 1956). Unfortunately, I did not gather enough samples to allow me to draw valid comparisons to data in Kloeke's study; it is not inconceivable, however, that a sufficiently great sample of data may someday be collected. For the time being, I can merely report that I have recorded virtually the entire spectrum of forms for southeastern speakers reported on 24–25, item no. 4, and must agree with Kloeke's overview statment made at that point: the area of *het* for *heeft* can be generally determined in the southeastern part of the Netherlands, but an exact epicenter of its use has not as yet been fixed (i.e., "het *het*-gebied van de Veluwe benevens het zuidelijk daarvan en het zuidelijk van de Oude IJsel liggende gebied kan ik voorlopig nog niet met . . . grote overtuiging als helemaal homogeen beschouwen").

17. For an overview of language blending and loan phenomena in situations of language contact such as those reported here, see Einar Haugen, "The Analysis of Linguistic Borrowing" in Haugen, *The Ecology of Language,* 79–109. See Van Hinte, *Netherlanders in America,* 996–97, for abundant examples of Americanized Dutch, including some instructive contrastive examples of sentences in North American and European Dutch.

18. Other examples of advertisements in hybrid languages are given by Lucas, *Netherlanders in America,* 582. For a very general list of English loan terms, see ibid., 582–83.

19. *Pella's Nieuwsbode* for June 30, 1899.

   Might the writer have been thinking of a form such as *manshoeden* 'men's hats', on the model of established forms such as *mansbroeken* 'men's pants'?

20. Ibid.

21. For examples of laughable misunderstandings, especially in correspondence, see Lucas, *Netherlanders in America,* 587–88.

22. Note the use of the auxiliary *zijn,* which would be required if the speaker were to use standard Dutch *beginnen.* Even if English vocabulary is penetrating the speaker's Dutch, certain basic grammatical categories remain Dutch.

23. Both *lijken* and *drijven* continue to take typically Dutch strong preterite and past participle forms with [e:]. Borrowed meaning does not necessarily mean borrowed morphological patterns.

Part Four

1. As a very general overview, one might wish to refer to Joshua A. Fishman, "Mother Tongue Claiming in the United States since 1960: Trends and Correlates Related to the 'Revival of Ethnicity'," *International Journal of the Sociology of Language* 50(1984): 21–99. Among the literally hundreds of possible studies that might be cited, I have chosen the following simply to represent the spectrum of topics and approaches: Patricia C. Nichols, "Creoles in America," in *Language in the USA*, edited by Charles A. Ferguson and Shirley Brice Heath, with the assistance of David Hwang (Cambridge: Cambridge University Press, 1981), 69–91; Dragon Milivojevic, "Language Maintenance and Language Shift in the United Slavonian Benevolent Association of New Orleans, Louisiana," *Melbourne Slavonic Studies* 18 (1984): 46–64; Arlene Malinowski, "Judeo-Spanish Language-Maintenance Efforts in the United States," *International Journal of the Sociology of Language* 44 (1983): 137–51.

2. Daan, "Language Use and Language Policy among Americans of Dutch Origin," 207–17; Guus Extra surveys linguistic minorities in the Netherlands and their treatment within the educational system in "Taalminderheden en onderwijs in vergelijkend perspektief," *Levende Talen* January 1982: 2–11; *Ethnic Minorities and Dutch as a Second Language*, ed. Guus Extra and Ton Vallen (Dordrecht: Foris, 1985); Elizabeth Sherman Swing, "Flemings and Puerto Ricans: Two Applicatons of a Conflict Paradigm in bilingual Education," *International Journal of the Sociology of Language* 44 (1983): 27–42. Those interested in Frisian will not want to miss the special issue of *Journal of the International Sociology of Language*, 64(1987), edited by Durk Gorter and devoted to "The Sociology of Frisian."

SELECT BIBLIOGRAPHY

Bratt, James D. *Dutch Calvinism in Modern America*. Grand
Rapids, Michigan: William B. Eerdmans, 1984.
_____."The Reformed Churches and Acculturation." In *The
Dutch in America. Immigration, Settlement and Cultural
Change*, edited by Robert P. Swieringa, 191–208. New
Brunswick, New Jersey: Rutgers University Press, 1985.
Bruins, Elton J. "Americanization in Reformed Religious Life."
In *The Dutch in America. Immigration, Settlement, and
Cultural Change*, edited by Robert P. Swierenga, 175–90.
New Brunswick, New Jersey: Rutgers University Press,
1985.
_____. *The Americanization of a Congregation. A History of
Third Reformed Church of Holland, Michigan*. The Histor-
ical Series of the Reformed Church in America, vol. 2.
Grand Rapids, Michigan: William. B. Eerdmans, 1970.
Clyne, Michael. "Nieuw-Hollands or Double-Dutch." *Dutch
Studies* 3(1977): 1–20.
Collins, Beverley, and Inger Mees. *The Sounds of Dutch and
English*. 2d ed. Leiden: E. J. Brill/Leiden University Press,
1984.
Daan, Jo. "Bilingualism of Dutch Immigrants in the U.S.A."
Actes du Xe congres international des linguistes I(1969):
759–63.
_____. "Bilingualism of Dutch Immigrants in the U.S.A." In
*Dichtung. Sprache. Gesellschaft. Akten des IV. interna-
tionalen Germanisten-Kongresses 1970 in Princeton*, edited

by Victor Lange and Hans-Gert Roloff, 205–13. Frankfurt: Athenaeum, 1971.

_____. *Ik was te bissie . . . Nederlanders en hun taal in de Verenigde Staten*. Zutphen: Walburg, 1987.

_____. "Language Use and Language Policy among Americans of Dutch Origin." In *Papers from the First Interdisciplinary Conference on Netherlandic Studies Held at the University of Maryland, 11–13 June 1982*, edited by William H. Fletcher, 207–17. Lanham, Maryland: University Press of America, 1985.

_____. "Verschuiven van isoglossen." *Taal en Tongval* 23 (1971): 77–80.

Daan, Jo, and D. P. Blok. *Van randstad tot landrand*. Amsterdam: North Holland, 1977.

Daan, Jo, Kas Deprez, Roeland van Houdt and Jan Stroop. *Onze veranderende taal*. Utrecht and Antwerp: Het Spectrum, 1985.

Daan, Jo, and K. Heeroma. *Zuidhollands*. Bijdragen en Mededelingen der Dialectcommissie van de Koninklijke Nederlandse Akademie van Wetenschappen te Amsterdam 30. Amsterdam: North Holland, 1965.

Dahm, James P., and Dorothy Van Kooten. *Peoria, Iowa. A Story of Two Cultures. 1853–1984*. Privately published, 1984.

Derr, Nancy. "The Babel Proclamation." *The Palimpsest* 60(1979): 98–115.

Deutekom, Peter van. (See Van Deutekom, Peter)

Dorian, Nancy C. *Language Death. The Life Cycle of a Scottish Gaelic Dialect*. Philadelphia: University of Pennsylvania Press, 1981.

Doyle, Richard L. "The Socio-Economic Mobility of the Dutch Immigrants to Pella, Iowa 1847–1925." Ph.D. dissertation, Kent State University, 1982.

Geerts, G., W. Haeseryn, J. de Rooij, and M. C. den Toorn, eds. *Algemene Nederlandse Spraakkunst*. Groningen: Wolters-Noordhoff; Louvain: Wolters, 1984.

Haugen, Einar. *The Ecology of Language. Essays by Einar Haugen*. Stanford: Stanford University Press, 1972.

_____. *The Norwegian Language in America. A Study in Bilingual Behavior.* Reprint (2 vols. in 1). Bloomington, Indiana and London: Indiana University Press, 1969.

Heeroma, K. *Hollandse dialektstudies.* Ph.D. dissertation, Royal University, Leiden. Groningen: J. B. Wolters, 1935.

Hinte, Jacob van. (see Van Hinte, Jacob)

A Historic Guide to Pella. Special tabloid of the *Pella Chronicle.* July 14, 1982.

Keizer, J. "De Nederlandsche Taal in Amerika." *De Gereformeerde Amerikaan* 4(1900): 503–5.

Klompenburg, Carol Van. (See Van Klompenburg, Carol)

Kooi, Muriel. *Festival. A Pictorial History of Tulip Time in Pella 1935–85.* Pella: Pella Historical Society, 1985.

Lieuwen, John. *Sweat and Tears.* Holland, Michigan: Steketee-Van Huis, 1947.

Lucas, Henry S. *Netherlanders in America. Dutch Immigration to the United States and Canada, 1789–1950.* Ann Arbor, Michigan: University of Michigan Press; London: Geoffrey Cumberlege and Oxford University Press, 1955.

Mulder, Arnold. *Americans from Holland.* Philadelphia and New York: J. B. Lippincott, 1947.

Nieland, Dirk. *'n fonnie bisnis.* Grand Rapids, Michigan: William B. Eerdmans, [1929].

Nollen, John. *De Hollanders in Iowa. Brieven uit Pella, van een Gelderschman.* Arnhem: D. A. Thieme, 1858.

Oostendorp, Lubbertus. *H. P. Scholte. Leader of the Secession of 1834 and Founder of Pella.* Th.D. dissertation, Free University of Amsterdam. Franeker: T. Wever, 1964.

Petersen, William. *Planned Migration. The Social Determinants of the Dutch-Canadian Movement.* University of California Publications in Sociology and Social Institutions 2. Berkeley and Los Angeles: University of California Press, 1955.

Pietersen, Lieuwe. *Taalsociologie. Minderheden. Tweetaligheid. Taalachterstand.* 2d ed. Groningen: Wolters-Noordhoff, 1980.

Roueché, Berton. "Pella, Iowa." In *Special Places: in Search of Small Town America,* 155–87. Boston and Toronto: Little, Brown, 1982.

_____. "Profiles: Oasis." *The New Yorker.* December 24, 1979, 46–68.

Schach, Paul, ed. *Languages in Conflict. Linguistic Accultura- tion on the Great Plains.* Lincoln, Nebraska, and London: University of Nebraska Press, 1980.

Schönfelds Historische Grammatica van het Nederlands. Pre- pared by A. van Loey with the collaboration of M. Schön- feld, rev. ed. Zutphen: W. J. Thieme, 1964.

Smit, Cornelis. *De Afscheiding van 1834.* 6 vols. Oudkarspel: De Nijverheid; Dordrecht: J. P. van den Tol, 1971–1984.

Smith, James Floyd. *Language & Language Attitudes in a Bilin- gual Community: Terherne (Friesland).* Grins/Groningen and Ljouwert/Leeuwarden: Frysk Ynstitut-Stabo/All- Round B.V.-Fryske Akademy, 1980.

Stellingwerff, J. *Amsterdamse emigranten. onbekende brieven uit de prairies van Iowa. 1846–1873.* Amsterdam: Buijten and Schipperheijn, 1975.

Stigt, K. van. (See Van Stigt, K.)

Stokvis, Pieter Rudolf Degenhard. *De Nederlandse trek naar Amerika. 1846–47.* Leiden: University Press, 1977.

Stout, G. A., compiler and publisher. *Souvenir History of Pella, Iowa.* Pella: The Booster Press, 1922. Reprint [1977].

Swierenga, Robert P. "Dutch." In *Harvard Encyclopedia of American Ethnic Groups,* edited by Stephen Thernstrom et al., 284–95. Cambridge, Massachusetts, and London: Har- vard University Press, 1980.

_____. "Exodus Netherlands, Promised Land America: Dutch Immigration and Settlement in the United States." In *A Bi- lateral Bicentennial. A History of Dutch-American Rela- tions, 1782–1982,* edited by J. W. Schulte Nordholt and Robert P. Swierenga. Amsterdam: Meulenhoff Interna- tional, 1982.

_____, ed. *The Dutch in America. Immigration, Settlement and Cultural Change.* New Brunswick, New Jersey: Rutgers University Press, 1985.

Teddern, Sue. "Another Netherlands." *Holland Herald* 17/4 (April 1982): 20–26.

Vander Werff, Dorothy D. L. "Evidence of Old Holland in the

Speech of Grand Rapids." *American Speech* 33(1958): 301–4.

Van der Zee, Jacob. *The Hollanders in Iowa.* Iowa City, Iowa: The State Historical Society of Iowa, 1912.

Van Deutekom, Peter. "Het Rijke Reformatorische Leven in Pella, Iowa. Yer not mutch, if yer not Dutch." *VU-Magazine* 10/2(February, 1981): 69–74.

Van Hinte, Jacob. *Netherlanders in America. A Study of Emigration and Settlement in the Nineteenth and Twentieth Centuries in the United States and Canada.* General editor Robert P. Swierenga; Adriaan de Wit chief translator. Reprint (2 vols. in 1). Grand Rapids, Michigan: Baker Book House, 1985.

Van Klompenburg, Carol. "Time out for Tulips." *The Iowan* Spring(1983): 4–13.

Van Stigt, K. *Geschiedenis van Pella, Iowa en omgeving.* Pella: Weekblad Print Shop, 1897. English transl. *History of Pella and Vicinity* by Elisabeth Kempkes published by the Central College Archivist, [1981].

Van Veen, T. *Utrecht tussen oost en west. Studies over het dialect van de provincie Utrecht.* Neerlandica Traiectina 14. Assen: Van Gorcum, 1964.

Veen, T. van. (See Van Veen, T.)

Veltman, Peter. "Dutch Survivals in Holland, Michigan." *American Speech* 15(February 1940): 80–83.

Vervoorn, A. J. *Antiliaans Nederlands.* The Hague: Kabinet voor Nederlands-Antiliaanse Zaken, n.d.

Wabeke, Bertus Harry. *Dutch Emigrants to North America 1624–1860. A Short History.* New York: The Netherlands Information Bureau, 1944.

Webber, Philip E. "Everyday Elaborations: Three Traditional Iowa Communities." In *Passing Time and Traditions,* edited by Steven Ohrn, 90–101. Ames: Iowa State University Press, 1984.

_____. "Nederlanders en Vlamingen in Iowa." *Ons Erfdeel* 23(1980) 458–60.

_____. "A Report on Ethnic Heritage and Language Education in Pella, Iowa." Prepared as a field report for the Ethnic

Heritage and Language Schools project of the American Folklife Center of the Library of Congress, 1982.

Webber, Philip E. and Garry Davis. "Bericht. Pella Dutch: Mogelijkheden voor Sociolinguïstisch Onderzoek." *Taal en Tongval* 31 (1979): 83–84.

Werff, Dorothy D. L. Vander. (See Vander Werff, Dorothy D. L.)

Wölck, Wolfgang. "Community Profiles: An Alternative Approach to Linguistic Informant Selection." *Linguistics* 177(1976): 4–57.

Zee, Jacob Van der. (See Van der Zee, Jacob)

INDEX

ABN. *See Algemeen beschaafd Nederlands*

Acculturation. *See* Americanization

Advantages of speaking Dutch. *See* Benefits of speaking Dutch

Age of sources, 18, 129, 136

Alcohol, 77

Algemeen beschaafd Nederlands (ABN), 84

Algemeen Nederlandsch Verbond, 54

American Folklife Center, 115

Americanization, 48–50, 55–60, 65–66; and national loyalty, 62–63; by post–World War II immigrants, 29, 67–68

"American Territory," 42

Architecture, local, 5, 121

Baden-Powell, Lord Robert, 61

Benefits of speaking Dutch, 32–33, 35

Bethel (neighborhood), 42

Birthplace of sources. *See* Sources, profile of

"Board of Dutch Education," 136

Boer War, ethnic solidarity during, 60–62

Buerkens, C. C., 9

Buurt. See Neighborhoods

Catechism: instruction in 22, 64. *See also* Heidelberg Catechism

Central College, 22, 51, 58–59;

Dutch Club, 66; sensitivity to heritage, 58–60

Childhood, recollections of, 29

Children's lore, 83–84, 136

Christian and public education. *See* Education in Christian and public schools

Churches and denominations, 12, 58, 122–23; Christian Reformed Church, 12, 22, 42, 53, 136; Darbyites, 12, 65; Reformed Church in America, 22, 42, 49, 58; Soul Sleepers, 12. *See also* Religion and language

Community values. *See* Values, community

Corporations, 5, 51

Costumes, of immigrants, 52, 56, 119

Cursing and strong language, 23, 27–28, 87

Daan, Jo, 102

Dancing, 47, 77

Darbyites. *See* Churches and denominations

Davis, Garry, 16

Derr, Nancy, 63, 64

De Somer, Gail Vande Bunte. *See* Vande Bunte-De Somer, Gail

Dialect: selecting informants for study of, 15; vestiges of in Pella Dutch, 88–92. *See also* Names, pronunciation of

Dorian, Nancy C., 13–14, 101

Lake Prairie District, 44

Language. *See inter al.* Cursing and strong language; Dialect; English; Fluency; Humor; Literacy; Maintenance of Dutch in Pella; Obsolescent languages; Pella Dutch; Religion and language; Schizoglossia; Yankee Dutch

Le Cocq, Ed, 80

Le Cocq, John F., 50

Leighton, Iowa, 42

Lewis, E. Glyn, 14

Liberty Bonds, sale of, 62

Limburg. *See* Dialect, vestiges of in Pella Dutch

Literacy: reading, 28–29, 31–32, 59; writing, 28, 31–32. *See also* Catechism, instruction in

Literal translations from English to Dutch. *See* English, influence on Dutch

Loan homonyms, 97–98

McKinley, William, President of the United States, 61

Maintenance of Dutch in Pella, 33–34, 131–35

Marriage partner selection, 57–58

Moral admonitions, 82

Music and heritage education, 120–21, 127–29

Names: etymologized, 10; family names, 9–10; given names, 10–11; nicknames, 11–12; in phone book, 12; pronunciation of, 10

Neighborhoods, 42–45; Earring District, 52

New Sharon, Iowa, 42

Newspapers and journalism: 9, 51–67 passim; ads in English, 56, 59; coverage of South Africa, 61–62; *Des Moines Capital*, 91; *Des Moines Register*, 64; *Pella*

Chronicle, 45; *Pella Gazette*, 48; *The Pella Press*, 46–47; *Pella's Weekblad*, 51, 53, 56, 66, 67; *De Sheboygan Nieuwsbode*, 50; *De Wachter*, 28; and World War I, 62–64. *See also* Buerkens, C. C.; Solano

Nicknames, 11–12

Obsolescent languages: indicators of, 21–22, 24–26; personality type of final speakers of, 74–75; research problems posed by, 17

Occupational patterns, 18, 59–60; and language use, 23, 75

Olivet (neighborhood), 42

Oskaloosa, Iowa, 42

Otley, Iowa, 42

Path of Delft, The, 124–27

Pella, Iowa, origin of name, 5, 118

Pella Dutch: adjectival forms, 86; characteristics of, 75–98; diminutive forms in, 87, 97; distinct from Standard Dutch, 17, 53, 66–67, 73, 84, 130; English influence on, 92–98; English words with Dutch forms, 95–98; literal translations from English, 92–93, 95; loan homonyms, 97–98; loanwords, 93–95; noun patterns, 85–86, 93–94, 95; perceived as old-fashioned, 73–74, 76, 120; phonological processes, 84, 96–98; pronominal forms, 86–87; used as a secret language, 30–31, 32, 74–75; verb patterns, 85, 94–95, 97–98, 130. *See also* Dialects, vestiges of in Pella Dutch; English, Dutch influences on

Pella Rolscreen. *See* Corporations

Peoria, Iowa, 22, 34, 42, 132, 133

Personality type of final speakers. *See* Obsolescent languages,

Vande Bunte-De Somer, Gail, 16
Van Raalte, A. C., 48
Vermeer Manufacturing Corporation.
  See Corporations
Voting, 62–64

Wabash line, debate over, 51
Weather lore, 79–81
Weekblad. See Newspapers and
  journalism, *Pella's Weekblad*
Wilson, Woodrow, President of the
  United States, 63
Workplace, use of language at. *See*

Occupational patterns and
  language use
World War I, 62–67, 119
World War II, 67, 119
Writing. *See* Literacy

Yankee Dutch, 9, 23, 130, 132
YMCA fund drives, 62
Young, Lafayette (Lafe), Sr., 64

Zeeland, province. *See* Dialect,
  vestiges of in Pella Dutch